THE ANATOMY SERIES OF INTERNATIONAL INSTITUTIONS

An Anatomy of the
World Trade Organization

THE ANATOMY SERIES OF INTERNATIONAL INSTITUTIONS

An Anatomy of the World Trade Organization

Edited by

Konstantinos Adamantopoulos
Head of the Hammond Suddards
International Trade Unit

HAMMOND SUDDARDS

SOLICITORS

KLUWER LAW INTERNATIONAL

LONDON – THE HAGUE – BOSTON

Published by
Kluwer Law International Ltd
Sterling House
66 Wilton Road
London SW1V 1DE
United Kingdom

Sold and distributed in
the USA and Canada by
Kluwer Law International
675 Massachusetts Avenue
Cambridge MA 02139
USA

Kluwer Law International Ltd
incorporates the publishing
programmes of Graham Trotman Ltd,
Kluwer Law and Taxation Publishers
and Martinus Nijhoff Publishers

In all other countries,
sold and distributed by
Kluwer Law International
P.O. Box 322
3300 Dordrecht
The Netherlands

ISBN 90-411-0711-8
Series ISBN 90-411-0735-5
© Kluwer Law International 1997
First Published 1997

British Library Cataloguing in Publication Data
A catalogue record for this book is available from the British Library

Library of Congress Cataloguing-in-Publication Data is available

Typeset in 10/12pt Veljovic by Oliver Hickey
Printed and bound in Great Britain by
Athenaum Press Ltd, Gateshead, Tyne and Wear.

CONTENTS

INTRODUCTION

"...the central role of the WTO, is the continued pursuit of assured, effective market access — worldwide ... — for traders, investors and inventors. That is and will remain the central objective. And while regional activities around the world, whether in Asia, Europe or the Americas, can and do contribute to trade liberalisation, our main tool for achieving that objective will be multilateral action. Bilateral approaches may achieve quicker results sometimes and, as Europe has shown itself in the internal market programme, regional initiatives can be the starting point for genuine worldwide liberalisation in new sectors. But many of the most serious problems our traders face today can only be tackled if all major trading partners act together.... the WTO is and must remain the motor of worldwide liberalisation."

Rt Hon Sir Leon Brittan, Vice-President of the European Commission, at the World Trade Congress, 24 April 1996.

PREFACE

Whilst it is the countries which are the members of the World Trade Organization ("WTO"), it is the companies which are its users. It is they who create international trade and are responsible for the resulting economic benefits. Therefore, it is important that companies understand how the WTO works, and what it does on their behalf. In the increasingly global market place information has become a priority for lawyers and business leaders.

It is with this in mind that Hammond Suddards has produced this anatomy of the WTO with the aim of providing a timely, precise and practical guide to the history, structure and functions of the WTO. The layout of the book, and the information it contains, have been presented in a way to make everyday use easy for those active in the international trade arena and to enable them to quickly pinpoint sources of information.

The book marks the first in a series of "anatomy" books written by Hammond Suddards and published by Kluwer Law International. Subsequent anatomy books will also focus on other international and European organisations.

Many people have contributed to the completion of this book and we are particularly grateful to Petros Mavroidis, a member of the WTO's Legal Service, for his comments and suggestions. The editor would also like to thank the following individuals: Stephen Tupper, Clive Martyr, Mariam John, Vassilis Akritidis, Jonathan Branton, Glynn Brassley, Clare Joyner, Clive Gordon and Oliver Pykett.

Anyone wishing further information regarding the World Trade Organization and International Trade Law, should contact:

Dr Konstantinos Adamantopoulos
Hammond Suddards, Avenue Louise 250, B- 1050 Brussels, Belgium

Tel: + 32 2 - 627 76 76
Fax: + 32 2 - 627 76 86
E-mail: kadamant@hammondsuddards.co.uk

LIST OF ABBREVIATIONS

ASEAN	Association of South East Asian Nations
ATC	Agreement on Textiles and Clothing
DSB	Dispute Settlement Body
DSU	Dispute Settlement Understanding
ECJ	European Court of Justice
ERG	Expert Review Group
EU	European Union
FDI	Foreign Direct Investment
GATS	General Agreement on Trade in Services
GATT	General Agreement on Tariffs and Trade
IEC	International Electrotechnical Commission
IMF	International Monetary Fund
IPR	Intellectual Property Rights
ITO	International Trade Organisation
MFA	Multi-Fibre Arrangement
MFN	Most Favoured Nation
NAFTA	North American Free Trade Agreement
OECD	Organisation for Economic Co-operation and Development
PGE	Permanent Group of Experts
SPS	Agreement on Sanitary and Phytosanitary Measures
TBT	Agreement on Technical Barriers to Trade
TMB	Textiles Monitoring Body
TPRM	Trade Policy Review Mechanism
TRIMS	Trade-Related Investment Measures
TRIPS	Trade-Related Aspects of Intellectual Property Rights
UNCTAD	United Nations Conference on Trade Development
USTR	United States Trade Representative
VER	Voluntary Export Restraint Arrangements
WTO	World Trade Organisation

A. HISTORY AND BACKGROUND

A.1 GATT and the multilateral trade negotiations

During the early 1930's, the world's leading trading nations were deep in recession. They reacted to the situation by introducing a series of highly protectionist measures. These measures, far from resolving the situation, merely served to undermine international trade.

Near the end of the Second World War, the United States and the United Kingdom, mindful of the negative consequences of uncontrolled trade protectionism, and seeking to avoid economic events of the 1930's, began to discuss plans for a post-war system of regulating world trade.

These bilateral discussions were broadened in 1946 when a Preparatory Committee was set up, under the auspices of the United Nations Economic and Social Council, to discuss and to produce a draft constitution for the International Trade Organisation ("ITO").

The ITO was intended, in conjunction with the World Bank and the International Monetary Fund ("IMF"), to form part of a trio of multinational organisations pledged to furthering economic development. More specifically, it was intended to put into place rules designed to discipline world trade whilst, in addition, implementing regulations relating to such diverse areas as employment, commodity agreements, restrictive business practices, international investment and services.

Whilst discussions about the ITO were taking place, a group of 23 participating countries began to negotiate a series of tariff concessions and certain free trade principles designed to prevent the introduction of restrictive measures amongst themselves.

During a six month period in 1947, significant tariff reduction negotiations were held which resulted in 45,000 binding tariff concessions

1

from the participant countries affecting about US $10 billion in trade. Pending the efforts for the establishment of the ITO, these binding tariff concessions and certain trade liberalisation principles became an integral part of the General Agreement on Tariffs and Trade ("GATT") signed in Geneva on 30 October 1947 by these 23 countries.

GATT was not intended to be a fully independent legal body. Its function was to act as an interim measure to put into effect the commercial policy provisions of the ITO. However, although 53 countries finally signed the ITO Charter in March 1948, the decision of the US Congress to vote against its ratification left GATT as the sole ("interim") framework for regulating and liberalising world trade.

The GATT mandate was to oversee international trade in goods and to gradually liberalise that trade by means of progressive reductions in tariff barriers. The furthering of trade liberalisation was to be achieved by negotiation "Rounds" held between various GATT contracting parties on a regular basis. In all, there have been eight GATT Rounds, including the Uruguay Round. A brief description of each Round is set out below (see Table A) accompanied by a table charting GATT's progress historically (see Tables B and C).

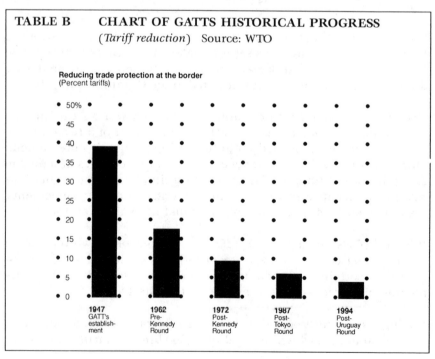

TABLE B   CHART OF GATT'S HISTORICAL PROGRESS
(*Tariff reduction*)   Source: WTO

Reducing trade protection at the border
(Percent tariffs)

| 1947 GATT's establishment | 1962 Pre-Kennedy Round | 1972 Post-Kennedy Round | 1987 Post-Tokyo Round | 1994 Post-Uruguay Round |

TABLE A CHRONOLOGY OF THE GATT ROUNDS

Year	Round	Activities
1947	Geneva	• 23 founder contracting parties • 45,000 tariff concessions agreed, covering US$10 billion in trade • Commitment to future negotiating "Rounds"
1949	Annecy	• Contracting parties exchange some 5,000 tariff concessions • Entry approved for 10 new GATT contracting parties
1951	Torquay	• 8,700 tariff concessions agreed leading to an overall tariff reduction of approximately 25% in relation to the 1947/48 level • Entry approved for four new GATT contracting parties
1956	Geneva	• US$2.5 billion of tariff reductions agreed
1960 – 1961	Geneva (Dillon Round)	• Single schedule of concessions agreed for the recently established European Economic Community, based on its Common External Tariff • 4,400 tariff concessions agreed covering US$4.9 billion of trade
1964 – 1967	Geneva (Kennedy Round)	• GATT membership now raised to 50 contracting parties, who account for 75% of world trade • Negotiations expanded, from a product-by-product approach to an industry/sector-wide method of cutting tariffs • A 50% cut in tariffs achieved in many areas — tariff concessions covered an estimated total trade value of $40 billion • Separate agreements concluded on grains and chemical products • Establishment of a Code on Anti-Dumping
1973 – 1979	Geneva (Tokyo Round)	• 99 countries participated • Tariff reductions and bindings agreed covering more than US$300 US$300 billion of trade • Average tariff on manufactured goods in the world's nine major industrial markets reduced from 7% to 4.7% • Agreements reached on: technical barriers to trade; subsidies and countervailing measures; import licensing procedures; government procurement; customs valuation; trade in bovine meat, dairy products and civil aircrafts; and a revised anti-dumping code
1986 – 1993	Geneva (Uruguay Round)	• 125 countries participated • Revision and strengthening of GATT rules; "Gatt 1994" • Substantial reductions in tariffs on trading goods • For the first time trade-related investment measures, trade in services and intellectual property rights become the subject of multilateral negotiations resulting in specific agreements • Establishment of the WTO (equipped with a strengthened Dispute Settlement Mechanism)

3

The establishment of the WTO could bring the need for GATT "Rounds" to an end. In the future, discussions about the liberalisation of trade will be ongoing, under the day-to-day direction of the General Council of the WTO (see section B.5.2). Major policy decisions will then be adopted at the Ministerial Conference — the top tier of the WTO structure (see section B.5.1) — every two years. A new negotiations round may however be necessary if the broadening of the WTO to cover such areas as labour, standards, environment and competition is deemed desirable.

The setting-up of the WTO should, in time, permit a greater degree of liberalisation of trade than under the GATT "Round" system of negotiations and with less of the accompanying trauma. The General Council, its sub-Councils and Committees (see sections B.5.2 — B.5.4) will be permanently engaged in monitoring and rendering effective the Uruguay Round Trade Agreements. As part of their function, they will discuss ways of further improving world trade. Although the General Council cannot itself take major policy decisions, it can discuss and instigate discussion about them. The advantage of this continuous negotiating forum is that by the time the Ministerial Conference takes place (every two years), many ideas for liberalising trade will already have been thoroughly debated and a consensus agreed. These strengthened WTO structures will make it easier for final decisions to be made at the Ministerial Conference itself. It was precisely this lack of advance planning and consensus that caused the later GATT rounds to become increasingly tied down and contentious.

A.2 *The Uruguay Round and its achievements*

The primary reason for holding the Uruguay Round was to further liberalise and thus ensure the continued existence of the international trade system established under GATT.

Despite overseeing a ninefold increase in world trade between 1947 and 1985, it was clear by the mid-1980's that a major review and modernisation of GATT was required in order to enable it to continue to successfully regulate the global market in the 21st century.

The goals of the Uruguay Round were:

- to achieve further liberalisation of trade by reducing tariffs and other barriers to trade;

- to properly reflect the modern developments in world trade by including in GATT negotiations for the first time trade-related investment measures, trade in services (20% of global trade) and intellectual property rights protection;

- to bring an end to exemptions of the GATT rules such as those granted to the agricultural clothing and textiles sectors, and so re-submit them to GATT discipline;

- to phase out all "voluntary export restraint arrangements" or "VER's" (prevalent in industries such as steel, electrical goods and motor vehicles) whereby one country agreed to limit its exports to another country to a pre-set level. Compliance of such arrangements with GATT has always been doubted. However, these arrangements have been long tolerated by GATT due to the economic and social significance of the sectors concerned; and

- to improve and strengthen the GATT dispute settlement procedure in order to ensure application of GATT rules and thus render it effective and credible.

"GATT 1994" is an updated and strengthened version of "GATT 1947" (the original GATT agreement). Unless otherwise stated, references to GATT are to GATT 1994. It forms part of the Uruguay Round Agreements and thus remains as the framework for the regulation and liberalisation of international trade. The four main tiers of GATT policy were and remain:

- the implementation of tariff bindings through an elaborate machinery for obtaining tariff concessions via multilateral trade negotiations and a system of registration of the concessions thus achieved;

- the general elimination of quantitative restrictions and a number of other important non-tariff barriers;

- the Most-Favoured-Nation ("MFN") treatment obligation for all GATT signatories (namely the requirement to treat products imported from different trading partners on the same basis); and

- the national treatment principle mandating equal treatment of domestic and imported products.

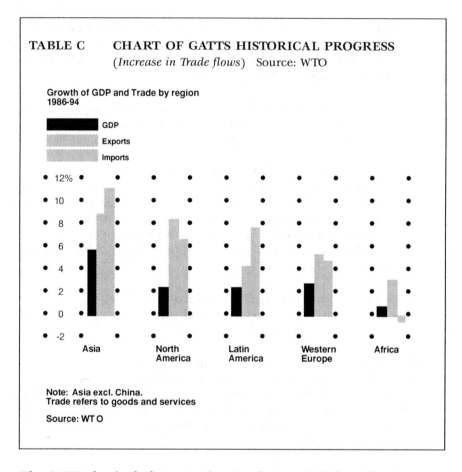

TABLE C   CHART OF GATTS HISTORICAL PROGRESS
(Increase in Trade flows)   Source: WTO

Growth of GDP and Trade by region
1986-94

GDP
Exports
Imports

Note: Asia excl. China.
Trade refers to goods and services

Source: WT O

The GATT also includes exceptions to these principles, allowing contracting parties to adopt "safeguards" and other measures, for example,
against dumping or subsidisation practices, which aim at correcting
undue imbalances of free trade. A number of agreements interpreting
related Articles of the 1947 GATT concluded during the various GATT
Rounds supplement the "GATT system". In addition, Article XXIV of
GATT enables GATT contracting parties to establish the trade areas
and customs unions among themselves without being obliged to
extend the preferential treatment granted thereof to all other GATT
contracting parties which are not parties to such arrangements.

In order to properly understand the WTO it is first necessary to provide an outline description of the GATT Uruguay Round which led to
its establishment and whose implementation it will carry out. The
final Uruguay Round Agreement comes to some 600 pages, with an

additional 25,000 pages of national tariff and services schedules, and therefore we have limited ourselves to a brief, overall description of its most important changes.

The contracting parties concluded eighteen separate agreements during the Uruguay Round. Each is described in outline terms in the list below. Fourteen of the agreements are multilateral and four are plurilateral. The multilateral agreements are binding on all Members of the WTO (countries which are signatories to the WTO are known as "Members"; previously GATT signatories were known as "Contracting Parties") whereas the plurilateral agreements, although administered by the WTO, are binding only between their signatories.

TABLE D   URUGUAY ROUND AGREEMENTS

MULTILATERAL	PLURILATERAL
1. Agriculture	1. Public Procurement
2. Sanitary and Phytosanitary Measures	2. Trade in Civil Aircraft
	3. International Dairy Products
3. Textiles and Clothing	4. International Bovine Meat
4. Technical Barriers to Trade	
5. Trade Related Investment Measures ("TRIMs")	
6. Anti-dumping	
7. Customs Valuation	
8. Pre-shipment Inspections	
9. Rules of Origin	
10. Import Licensing Procedures	
11. Subsidies and Countervailing Measures	
12. Safeguards	
13. General Agreement on Trade in Services ("GATS")	
14. Trade Related Intellectual Property ("TRIPS")	
15. Dispute Settlement	
16. Trade Policy Review Mechanism ("TPRM")	

Except as otherwise provided, the term "Member" in this bookrefers to a country that has agreed to the terms of the Uruguay Round Multilateral Trade Agreements and has acceded to the WTO.

A.2.1   Agriculture

Agriculture has traditionally been one of the most contentious areas of world trade. Prior to the Uruguay Round, it was subject to a series of agreements that effectively put it outside the GATT sphere of influence.

The sector proved to be the most difficult to negotiate during the Uruguay Round. Indeed, the unwillingness of major developed nations such as the United States and the European Union to make concessions almost led to its collapse. In the end, intensive negotiations, common sense and considerable pressure (from the Australian led CAIRNS Group of agricultural products exporting countries) led to an agreement which significantly liberalised agricultural trade. The main agreement, which includes the establishment of a Committee on Agriculture (see section B.5.4.1), can be divided up into three sections:

- market access;
- domestic support; and
- export subsidies.

Each are discussed in greater detail below:

A.2.1.1 Market Access

The following major changes to the system of rules governing market access have been agreed (it should be noted that only GATT contracting parties benefit from these changes – new signatories to the WTO do not):

- All measures directly affecting imports of agricultural products other than customs duties (for example, agricultural levies) are to be converted into customs duties ("tariffication").

- Tariffs arising from the new "tariffication" process along with other tariffs on agricultural products are to be reduced by an average of (i) 36% in six years from 1995 for developed countries; and (ii) 24% in ten years from 1995 for developing countries. No reduction is required in the case of the least developed countries.

● A special safeguard clause permits a country, under strictly defined conditions, to maintain import restrictions to the end of the six or ten year implementation period.

● For those products for which few or no imports took place as a result of the restrictive nature of the pre-existing regime, minimum access opportunity commitments have been made, representing not less than 3% of domestic consumption in the base period 1986–88, rising to 5% of that base figure by the end of the various implementation periods.

A.2.1.2 Domestic Support

Members have made an undertaking to cut the overall level of internal market support (ie national schemes for maintaining domestic prices at high levels and/or direct subsidies) to farmers by the following amounts:

● developed countries – 20% over six years;

● less developed countries – 20% over ten years; and

● least developed countries – no change.

So-called "Green Box" policies are excluded from the undertaking. Green Box policies include general government services (such as research, infrastructure, food safety and disease control) as well as direct payments to producers in the form of special income support, structural adjustment assistance, direct payments under environmental programmes and regional assistance programmes.

A.2.1.3 Reductions in Export Subsidies

The level of direct export subsidies is to be reduced as follows:

● developed countries — to a level of 36% below that of the 1986/90 base period over six years;

● less developed countries — as per the developed countries but over ten years; and

● least developed countries — no change.

A.2.2 Sanitary and Phytosanitary

Although sanitary and phytosanitary measures have been generally covered by GATT since 1947, whether under GATT's own Articles (particularly XX: b) or as a result of other trade agreements (ie the Tokyo Round Agreement on Technical Barriers to Trade), there has never been a specific sector agreement until now. However, this left governments concerned that without specific regulation of the sanitary and phytosanitary sector sanitary and phytosanitary measures might be increasingly used as a disguised, but deliberate, alternative means of restricting trade. The new Uruguay Round Agreement in this area tackles this risk by setting out detailed requirements for the use of sanitary and phytosanitary measures whilst preserving the rights of governments to implement food safety, animal and plant regulations in circumstances where they are necessary to protect human, animal or plant life. More specifically:

- measures should not be used to discriminate in an arbitrary/unjustifiable manner against other Members where identical or similar conditions exist;

- harmonisation is encouraged — signatories of the agreement are encouraged to base measures on internationally recognised standards, where they exist;

- the introduction or maintenance of higher standards by Member States can be justified on scientific grounds or where appropriate risk assessment procedures have been followed. A dispute procedure exists where other Member States feel that higher standards are being used as an excuse for market protection;

- an obligation of transparency has been established — Member States must publish all sanitary and phytosanitary measures taken; and

- a Committee on Sanitary and Phytosanitary Measures has been established to monitor the Agreement (see section B.5.4.2).

A.2.3 Textiles and Clothing

As with agriculture, the textile and clothing sector has proved to be a major source of discord over the years between the developed and less developed countries. The 1974 Multi-Fibre Arrangement ("MFA") had effectively removed textiles and clothing from the GATT framework, to the often considerable disadvantage of the least developed trading nations. The Uruguay Round negotiations have succeeded in returning the clothing and textile sector to the GATT fold. The following has been agreed:

- MFA and non-MFA restrictions (ie those not negotiated in the framework of GATT) are to be phased out in four stages, with fixed percentages of products to be integrated at each stage. The first stage became operational on 1 January 1995 and required Member States to immediately integrate into GATT no less than 16% of their 1990 total volume of imports of textiles and clothing. The second stage beginning on 1 January 1998 will see the integration of a further 17% of products, with an additional 18% on 1 January 2002 and the remaining 49% on 1 January 2005;

- during the course of the phasing out process, those products which still remain subject to restrictions are to benefit from fixed rates of growth in their quota levels. During the first phase (January 1995 – December 1997) the annual growth of each quantitative restriction still in force will be no less than 16 per cent. In the second phase (January 1998 – December 2001) the quantitative restrictions will be increased by a further 25 per cent with an additional increase of 27 per cent in the third phase (January 2002 – December 2004); and

- safeguards will be available to those countries whose domestic industries may suffer in the short term as a consequence of the removal of restrictions. The safeguards can be agreed bilaterally or imposed unilaterally but must not reduce the volume of trade below the actual level of exports or imports from the country concerned during the previous twelve month period. However, they will be subject to strict monitoring by the Textiles Monitoring Body (see section B.5.4.3) and will, in any event, only be available for a maximum three-year period.

A.2.4 Technical Barriers to Trade

The Agreement on Technical Barriers to Trade strengthens and clarifies a previous agreement reached during the Tokyo Round. The new agreement accepts that all countries have the right to introduce such regulations and standards as they consider necessary in order to ensure health and safety and to protect the environment. It is, however, also important to ensure that technical regulations do not in reality create unnecessary barriers to trade. The new agreement, which covers all products, including industrial and agricultural products:

- requires Members who are preparing, adopting or applying a technical regulation which may significantly affect the trade of other Members to justify the regulation upon request from affected Members;

- encourages Members to co-operate (with a view to harmonisation on as wide a basis as possible) in the preparation by international standardising bodies of international standards for products for which they have adopted, or expect to adopt, technical regulations;

- states that Members should try to accept equivalent technical regulations of other Members, even when they differ, in cases where those regulations effectively fulfil the objectives set out in their own regulations;

- stipulates that wherever appropriate Members should specify technical regulations based on product requirements in terms of performance as opposed to design or descriptive characteristics;

- provides a notification procedure where no relevant international standard exists or where a proposed technical regulation does not accord with international standards and where the new regulation may have a significant effect on the trade of other Members. In particular, the procedure states that Members should:

  (i)   publish well in advance a notice of the proposed technical regulation;

  (ii) notify other Members (through the WTO Secretariat) of the products covered by the regulation, as well as an indication of its objective;

  (iii) provide copies of the proposed regulation to other Members on request, identifying the elements of the regulation that vary from international standards;

(iv) allow time for written comments to be made by other Members and take into account these and any discussions held before finalising the regulation; and

(v) promptly make the newly adopted regulation available to other Members or interested parties;

● introduces a Code of Good Practice for the Preparation, Adoption and Application of Standards, comprising all the above mentioned points. According to the Code, Members must ensure that their central government standardising bodies covered by this Code:

   (i) publish a work programme every six months containing their names and addresses and the standards they are currently preparing or have adopted in the preceding period; and

   (ii) lodge their work programme with the IEC (International Electrotechnical Commission) Information Centre in Geneva;

● establishes a Committee on Technical Barriers to Trade (see section B.5.4.4).

A.2.5 Trade-Related Investment Measures

Foreign Direct Investment ("FDI") is a significant area of growth in the global economy and one of particular importance to the European Union ("EU"). Recent figures claim that 36% of worldwide FDI inflow originates from the EU and that the EU receives 19% of world FDI inflow. It is a result of the increase in FDI that Trade-Related Investment Measures ("TRIMS") were included for the first time in the Uruguay Round.

Whilst not aimed at protecting and establishing multilateral rules on FDI the new agreement nevertheless recognises that certain national measures attach conditions on FDI which result in a restriction and distortion of trade. The TRIMS agreement, therefore, implements Articles III:5 and XI of the GATT in this section and sets out to clarify what measures are and are not permissible. It includes a long list of prohibited measures such as those which require particular levels of local procurement by an enterprise or which restrict the volume or value of imports that such an enterprise can purchase.

In general, the following are listed as prohibited TRIMS:

- requirements to purchase from domestic sources;

- limitations on the purchase or use of imported products tied to the volume or value of local products exported;

- restrictions on importation whether or not tied to the volume or value of local production exported;

- restrictions on importation effected by limiting foreign exchange to an amount related to foreign exchange earnings; and

- restrictions on exportation or sale for export.

The TRIMS agreement increases transparency by requiring the notification of all existing prohibited measures to the WTO Secretariat. It further requires that these measures be removed within the following time scales:

- developed countries — two years.
- developing countries — five years.
- least developed countries — seven years.

In addition, a Committee on TRIMS is to be established (see section B.5.4.5). Its responsibilities will include the monitoring and implementation of the above commitments.

A.2.6 Anti-Dumping

Anti-dumping measures are frequently used and highly contentious. Although GATT provided for the right of its contracting parties to impose such measures, its provisions are frequently criticised as lacking the clarity required to prevent evasion and abuse of the rules. The new agreement seeks to remedy this situation. Significant changes include:

- acceptance of the principle that firms may under certain conditions, during their start-up period, sell up to 20% of their production at a loss;

- clarification of the rules relating to anti-dumping procedures and the conduct of investigations. The new rules largely reflect long-established EU practices;

● introduction of a "sunset" clause which will result in a five-yearly review of all anti-dumping actions;

● inclusion of a "de minimis" rule which will terminate anti-dumping actions against small volume imports or those that produce a negligible effect on trade;

● implementation of new rules relating to the tabling of complaints — complainants must, in most cases, represent a majority of domestic producers in the relevant market. In certain circumstances complainants representing 75% to 50% of the market may table complaints; and

● establishment of a Committee on Anti-Dumping Practices (see Section B.5.4.6).

A.2.7 Customs Valuation

Customs valuation is a complex component of the world trade system, and one that has proved particularly susceptible to fraudulent practices. The new agreement represents a strengthened version of the Tokyo Round's first attempt to regulate this aspect of trade. The agreement:

● re-emphasises that the basis for valuation of goods for customs purposes should, to the maximum extent possible, be the transaction value of the goods being valued;

● gives customs administrations:

(i) additional powers to request further information from importers if they doubt the accuracy of the declared value of imported goods; and

(ii) the right and obligation to establish the customs value by having recourse to alternative methods provided in the agreement, where, despite additional information, the customs administration still doubts the declared value of the goods; and

● establishes a Committee on Customs Valuation to oversee the administration of the agreement (see section B.5.4.7).

A.2.8 Pre-Shipment Inspections

This involves the use of specialised private companies to check shipment details such as the price, quantity and quality of goods ordered overseas. They are used principally as a means of protecting the national interest (ie prevention of illegal movements of capital, commercial fraud, customs duty evasion) by the developing countries.

The agreement applies GATT principles and obligations, in particular, those of non-discrimination and transparency to the carrying out of pre-shipment inspections mandated by governments. An independent review procedure to resolve disputes between pre-shipment inspection agencies and exporters is to be established.

The procedure will be administered by an independent body consisting of a combination of separate organisations representing exporters and agencies. At the request of a complainant (exporter or agency) the independent body will establish a panel of experts from an existing list. The panel will consist of three experts, one each nominated by the individual organisations representing exporters and agencies and one independent expert, nominated by the administration body itself. The independent expert will act as chairman. The panel will determine if both parties to the dispute fully complied with the rules. Parties may present their views to the panel in person or in writing. The panel must make its decision by majority vote within eight days of the request for a review. The decision is binding on the parties to the dispute.

A.2.9 Rules of Origin

Origin is the "nationality" of a product. The problem of how to define what constitutes a country of origin has long perplexed the trading world. This issue has become increasingly important as the various stages of the manufacture of products increasingly take place in more than one country. The origin of a product determines the product's treatment in an importing country (ie the amount of customs duties; the granting of preferential treatment; the imposition of anti-dumping duties; the free circulation of a product in a free trade area, etc.).

The new agreement on Rules of Origin attempts to impose a sense of order on this difficult component of world trade.

The object of the agreement is to achieve a long term harmonisation of the rules of origin (with the exception of those rules relating to the granting of tariff preferences) and to ensure that the rules do not in themselves create unnecessary barriers to trade. Certain basic principles identifying, in general terms, manufacturing stages conferring origin on the final product are set out. So, for example, as a general rule and for non-preferential trade purposes a product originates in the country where the last substantial processing or manufacturing took place. A value-added test (generally between 40–45%) with regard to the last country of processing on manufacturing may also be used.

A Committee on Rules of Origin in GATT (see section B.5.4.8), in conjunction with a subsidiary technical committee is to supervise the harmonisation of various countries' product-specific origin rules procedure. This ambitious harmonisation process is due to be completed within three years. Until harmonisation is completed, Members are expected to ensure that their rules of origin are transparent as well as positive in nature (ie stating what does confer origin on a certain product rather than the reverse).

A.2.10 Import Licensing Procedures

Import licensing is a means of checking the level of imports coming into a particular country. It helps to ensure that only legally permitted goods enter and that quota limits are not exceeded. The revised Tokyo Round agreement tightens the rules governing users of import licensing systems as well as increasing transparency and predictability. In particular:

- sufficient information must be published by importing countries to enable traders to understand the basis on which licences are granted;

- increased guidance is now provided on the assessment of licence applications;

- in order to avoid unnecessary and potentially costly delays, licence applications must be considered within a maximum of 60 days;

ANATOMY OF THE WTO

- any Member wishing to introduce new licensing procedures, or alter existing ones, must notify the Committee on Import Licensing (see section B.5.4.9) who will then publish them within 21 days; and

- criteria have been set out specifying the circumstances under which "automatic" licensing procedures (under which approval of the application is always granted) are considered not to restrict trade and stating that, in the case of "non-automatic" licensing procedures, the administrative burden imposed on importers and exporters should be kept to the bare working minimum.

A.2.11 Subsidies and Countervailing Measures

Subsidies constitute a means for the sovereign exercise of economic, social and development policy, but frequently result in distortions of trade, due to their impact on prices. Problems can be settled either through domestic regulation or by directly approaching the WTO for multilateral dispute resolution. The Subsidies Agreement builds on earlier negotiations and the agreement reached during the Tokyo Round. Major changes include:

- agreement for the first time on the definition of subsidy and, more particularly, of the term "specific subsidy". Only "specific subsidies" are governed by the agreement and refer to those subsidies that are available only to an enterprise or industry (or a group of enterprises or industries) operating within the jurisdiction of the granting authority;

- the categorisation of "specific subsidies" as follows:

  (i) *prohibited* — those subsidies which are conditional in law or practice upon export performance or upon the use of domestic rather than imported goods. Any country introducing such a subsidy will be referred to the Dispute Settlement Body (see section B.14). If the subsidy is confirmed as being prohibited then the responsible country must withdraw it immediately. Failure to do so within an allotted period of time may result in the imposition of retaliatory and countervailing measures;

(ii) *actionable* — those subsidies which, although not prohibited, adversely affect other Members and seriously prejudice their interests. Serious prejudice will be presumed where the ad valorem subsidisation of a product exceeds 5% or, where a subsidy has been given in order to prop up a loss-making industry. Where serious prejudice is cited by a Member, the burden of proof is on the subsidising Member to show that this is not the case. The affected Member has the right to refer an unresolved dispute to the Dispute Settlement Body where a finding of serious prejudice will result in the subsidy having to be withdrawn, or, the prejudicial part of it removed. In addition, the Member suffering injury thereby may adopt countervailing measures;

(iii) *non-actionable* — those subsidies which assist industrial research and pre-competitive development activity, provide assistance to disadvantaged regions or are used in certain circumstances to assist in adapting existing facilities to new environmental requirements. In the event that a Member believes that a non-actionable subsidy is having an adverse effect on its domestic industry it may refer the matter to the Committee on Subsidies and Countervailing Measures (see section B.5.4.10) for a review and binding recommendations and may, eventually, adopt countervailing measures;

- introduction of new compulsory rules on the calculation of the value of subsidies;

- recourse to an expedited disputes procedure under the Disputes Settlement Mechanism (see section B.14);

- the stipulation that a subsidy must have an effect on trade to come within the remit of the WTO; and

- the authorising of least developed and developing countries, namely those with less than $1000 per head Gross National Products, to use otherwise "prohibited" export subsidies, and to have time-bound exemptions from other prohibited subsidies.

A.2.12 Safeguards

Safeguard clauses are an allowable protective measure designed to shield domestic industries from sudden and unexpected increases in imports whenever such imports cause or threaten to cause serious injury to domestic industry. This generally takes the form of quantitative import restrictions ("import quotas"), import surveillance measures (through the imposition of import licensing procedures), or the imposition of high customs duties. The Safeguards Agreement attempts to strengthen the effectiveness of safeguard measures whilst at the same time limiting both their scope and duration. Important changes include:

- phasing out all "grey area" measures such as voluntary export restraints ("VER's") agreements and orderly market arrangements. However, one VER per member will be tolerated over a specific period of time provided it has been notified to the WTO;

- the establishment of a Committee on Safeguards (see section B.5.4.11) to monitor all safeguard measures taken and to ensure their compliance with the agreement;

- the restriction of safeguard measures to a maximum four year period, with the possibility of one four-year extension. Measures in existence prior to the Uruguay Round are to be phased out by the end of 1999;

- for the first time, the possibility of taking selective action against individual countries where their exports are thought to be particularly damaging; and

- recourse to the Dispute Settlement Mechanism (see section B.14) in the event of an enduring disagreement between Members.

A.2.13 General Agreement on Trade in Services ("GATS")

The Uruguay Round includes for the first time a "General Agreement on Trade in Services" (or "GATS") which attempts to do for services what GATT has done for trading goods by establishing a multilateral framework for the reduction and elimination of barriers to international trade in services. GATS establishes the Most Favoured Nation ("MFN") (equalisation of treatment) principle for trade in services, which, it is hoped, will lead to an improvement in the position of those countries currently subject to discrimination. As with other GATT/WTO elements, GATS contains a series of rules and specific commitments to open markets. Members of the new WTO are now obliged to offer MFN status and provide market access ensuring transparency to all service providers from countries bound by GATT. Exemptions to MFN can be sought in specific circumstances. For example, it should be noted that the EU has an MFN exemption in the audio-visual sector and, therefore, is not bound to give equal treatment to third countries.

The GATS agreement contains three elements:

- a framework of general rules and disciplines;

- annexes consisting of special conditions relating to individual sectors; and

- national schedules of market access commitments.

The GATS framework is made up of 29 articles. The scope of the agreement covers all internationally-traded services, however they are delivered. Services fall within one of four modes of delivery, namely:

- services supplied from one Member to another (ie international telephone calls);

- services supplied in the territory of one Member to the consumers of any other (ie tourism);

- services provided through the presence of a commercial entity of one Member in the territory of any other (e.g. banking); and

- services provided by individuals of one Member in the territory of any other (ie fashion models).

Whilst GATS intends to protect services it does not apply directly to services themselves but to governmental measures affecting trade in services. These "measures" can take the form of regulations, rules, procedures, decisions, administrative actions etc. and may be made by any level of government.

There are four GATS annexes, covering the movement of persons, financial services, telecommunications and air transport services. These annexes represent negotiations that were incomplete at the end of the Uruguay Round but were granted an extension of time.

Negotiations are currently still ongoing (see section C.8.5).

The national rules (which include MFN exemptions) contain the negotiated and guaranteed conditions under which international trade in services is conducted. Once recorded, such a national obligation cannot be adversely altered without three months advance notice of the change and the negotiation of compensation to affected countries. However, improvements to the schedules can be made at any time. In any event, Members are committed to further liberalisation of services under GATS by means of future negotiating sessions.

In summary, over 150 services and sub-sectors can be covered by the new rules, including professional services (accounting, architecture and engineering), other business services (computer services, rental and leasing, advertising and consulting), communications (telecommunications, audio visual services), construction, distribution (wholesale and retail trade, franchising), financial services (banking, securities, insurance) and others. Benefits will extend not only to service providers but also to entities that depend on accounting, financial, legal, insurance and other service providers to conduct their business.

A Council for Trade in Services (see section B.5.3.2) is established, entrusted with the task of furthering the objectives of the agreement. Given that detailed and difficult negotiations are still taking place over the scope of GATS, the Committee can expect to be particularly active in the coming months.

A.2.14 Trade-Related Intellectual Property

A significant and ever increasing volume of world trade is now regulated by Intellectual Property Rights ("IPR") in one form or another. As trading increases, so do incentives to breach IPR. Counterfeiting, copying and "piracy" are now widespread, thus presenting barriers to fair trade. The situation is exacerbated by the fact that such practices are not illegal in many of the less developed countries. The copying of products has led to a considerable loss of export revenue amongst the industrialised nations. The worst hit industries have been chemicals and pharmaceuticals, but other major problem areas include books, records, software and entertainment. It is estimated that the EU loses at least 10% of the value of its exports to copyright piracy. An additional problem has been the appropriation of brand names and even, in the case of wine and foodstuffs, geographical appellations. This, coupled with poor quality in the "secondary" product, has had damaging effects on the reputation of genuine articles.

As a result of these growing trends, Intellectual Property Rights were included in the Uruguay Round negotiations. The Trade-Related Intellectual Property ("TRIPs") agreement attempts to regulate and standardise international IPR in order to prevent the above-mentioned abuses and so create a fairer trade market. The result has seen a strengthening of existing international conventions, such as the Berne and Paris Conventions for the protection of literary and artistic works, by bringing them within the ambit of the WTO Dispute Settlement Mechanism. There has also been a strengthening of IPR in the following additional areas:

- stronger protection of trade marks;

- greater protection for industrial designs, especially within the textile and clothing industry;

- introduction of patent protection in all countries for pharmaceutical and chemical products;

- extension to a world-wide level of semiconductor protection;

- prohibition of appropriation and misuse of geographical appellations;

- establishment of a clear set of principles for the enforcement of IPR through the national courts. Breaches will be subject to sanctions under the Dispute Settlement Procedure;

- setting up of a Council for TRIPS (see section B.5.3.3) to oversee the smooth running of the agreement; and

- establishment of the rules on compulsory licensing necessary for developing countries.

A.2.15 Dispute Settlement

The establishment of a Dispute Settlement Mechanism was one of the major achievements of the Uruguay Round. A dispute settlement procedure existed in the pre-Uruguay Round GATT but it was handicapped by the refusal of countries, particularly the developed countries, to bring cases before it or, on those rare occasions, to respect its final rulings. The new Dispute Settlement Mechanism represents the "teeth" of the new WTO. The Members have, in the Uruguay Round Agreement, agreed not to take unilateral action, as so often occurred in the past against perceived violations of trade rules. Instead, they have pledged to seek recourse in the new system and to abide by its rules and procedures. The trade agreements acknowledge that prompt settlement of disputes is essential to the effective functioning of the WTO. The framework document for the Dispute Settlement Mechanism is contained in an Annex to the Uruguay Round Agreement entitled "Understanding on Rules and Procedures Governing the Settlement of Disputes" which updates a similar practice by the GATT Secretariat developed during the 1980's.

A comprehensive study of the structure, procedures and authority of the new Dispute Settlement Mechanism can be found under section B.14 of this book.

A.2.16 Trade Policy Review Mechanism

The purpose of the Trade Policy Review Mechanism ("TPRM") is to monitor the trade policies and practices of the WTO's Members and to assess their impact on the multilateral and, where relevant, plurilateral trading system. The aim of the TRPM is to achieve a greater degree of transparency and understanding of Member's trade policies which will lead to a smoother running of the global trade system (see section B.16).

A.2.17 Plurilateral Trade Agreements

The agreements on goods, services and IPR are grouped together under the heading "Multilateral Agreements". The significance of the Multilateral Agreements is that accession to the WTO is dependant on their acceptance in full by potential members. However, a number of other agreements whose acceptance is not a pre-requisite to WTO membership, were also concluded during the Uruguay Round. These "Plurilateral Agreements" were formally annexed to the Final Act of the Uruguay Round and will be regulated and supervised by the WTO. These agreements will, however, only be applicable (and thus enforceable), between their signatories.

There are four Plurilateral Agreements concerning (i) Public Procurement, (ii) Trade in Civil Aircraft; (iii) International Dairy Products; and (iv) International Bovine Meat Products.

A.2.17.1 *Public Procurement*

The new agreement on public procurement will supersede the current, limited, "Code" which has been in operation since 1981. The new agreement expands the Code in the following manner:

- the key feature of the new agreement on public procurement is that foreign suppliers and foreign goods and services must be given no less favourable treatment in government procurement than national suppliers of goods and services. To achieve this, tendering procedures have been revised and strengthened, as have rules relating to the qualifications of suppliers, the contents of tender documentation provided to those potential suppliers and the time limits for tendering and delivery. In addition, information explaining how and why a contract has been awarded is now mandatory;

- whereas the earlier Code only covered a limited number of central government departments, the new agreement includes additional government departments at a national and sub-national level, regional states, cantons and, in some cases, large metropolitan authorities;

- procurement for construction projects and services, as well as products, is now covered;

- additional countries have become signatories to the new agreement, taking the total to eight, in addition to the EU Member States;

- a Committee on Government Procurement under the supervision of the WTO General Council has been established; and

- private parties will be able, through the national courts, to challenge violations of the Code by parties to the agreement.

A.2.17.2   Trade in Civil Aircraft

The agreement, which has 21 signatories, was originally concluded during the Tokyo Round and came into force on 1 February 1980. Its major points include:

● the elimination of import duties on all aircraft (other than military aircraft), as well as on civil aircraft engines and their parts and components, all civil aircraft components and sub-assemblies as well as flight stimulators and their parts and components;

● the imposition of strict regulations to cover government directed procurement of civil aircraft (including inducements to purchase) as well as government financial support for the civil aircraft sector; and

● the establishment of a Committee on Civil Aircraft, under the supervision of the WTO General Council.

A.2.17.3   International Dairy Products

The International Dairy Arrangement became effective on 1 January 1980. The agreement, which covers all dairy products, aims to introduce greater stability in the market by seeking to limit surpluses, shortages and large fluctuations in price. In addition, the agreement:

● seeks to improve international co-operation in the dairy products sector;

● commits itself to assisting in the economic and social advancement of developing countries; and

● establishes an International Dairy Council, under the guidance of the WTO General Council, with responsibility for setting minimum export prices for trade in milk powders, milk fat (including butter), and certain cheeses.

A.2.17.4   International Bovine and Meat Products

Along with the Dairy and Civil Aircraft Agreements, the International

Bovine Meat Agreement, with 27 signatories including the EU, was originally negotiated during the Tokyo Round. The agreement, which covers beef, veal and live cattle, seeks an expanded but regulated market in meat and livestock. In particular the agreement:

- aims to improve international co-operation in the meat products sector; and

- establishes an International Meat Council under the guidance of the WTO General Council, to evaluate the world supply and demand situation for meat and to generally act as a forum for discussion on all matters relating to the bovine meat products sector of world trade.

B. THE WORLD TRADE ORGANIZATION

The results of the Uruguay Round, accompanied by the establishment of the WTO, represent a major reform in the operation of the world trading system.

Successful exploitation of the new system by companies will depend on the ability of companies to:

- exploit new markets for their products and services;

- respond to increased import competition;

- form strategic alliances and execute cross-border acquisitions and investment strategies; and

- monitor and participate in the implementation process of the Uruguay Round Agreements.

The first three points mentioned above fall outside the scope of this book, but the last point is particularly relevant, involving as it does the WTO.

The ability of a company to monitor and participate in the implementation process of the Uruguay Round Agreements is dependent on its understanding of how the WTO, which has responsibility for those functions, operates. With this need in mind, this section of the book aims to:

- clarify the differences between GATT and the WTO;

- detail the structure of the WTO and how its various component parts interrelate;

- demonstrate the importance of the Dispute Settlement Mechanism; and

- identify the manner and extent of a company's ability to deal with and/or influence the WTO.

Included is (i) basic contact information (see section B.4); (ii) charts illustrating the structure of the WTO; (iii) a description of its various councils and committees (see section B.5) and its secretariat (see section B.6); (iv) a description of the WTO's relationship to other multinational organisations (see section B.15).

B.1 *Basic Differences Between Gatt and WTO*

There are six major differences between GATT and the WTO:

- whereas the GATT framework allowed for the existence of a number of important side agreements negotiated and concluded by certain GATT contracting parties in the framework of the various GATT Rounds, the WTO administers a unified package of agreements to which all members are committed (ie the Uruguay Round Agreement now forms an integral part of the WTO);

- the WTO has considerably expanded the role of GATT by including Trade in Services and IPR within the multilateral trading system. In addition, the environment becomes a major agenda item for the first time;

- the WTO contains an improved version of the original GATT rules — "GATT 1994", which re-state and strengthen the original GATT rules concerning trade in goods;

- GATT trade opt-out agreements, such as those governing the clothing and textiles and agriculture sectors are to be gradually overturned and so-called "grey area" measures including voluntary arrangements and export restraints are to be phased out. Virtually all trade in goods will from now on be subject to GATT/WTO rules;

- the potential membership of the WTO of some 150 countries is far wider than under the GATT. This fact undoubtedly serves to strengthen the arm of the WTO; and

● WTO Members cannot block decisions arrived at under the dispute settlement mechanism. Under the GATT dispute panel findings were often blocked.

B.2   *Scope of the WTO*

The WTO is designed to provide a common institutional framework for the conduct of trade relations amongst its members relating to the Multilateral and Plurilateral Agreements arising from the Uruguay Round.

The Multilateral Agreements are binding on all Members of the WTO.

The Plurilateral Agreements, whilst administered by the WTO, are only binding on their signatories.

B.3   *Functions of the WTO*

The most important function of the WTO is to implement, administer, direct and further the objectives of the Multilateral and Plurilateral Trade Agreements resulting from the Uruguay Round. To achieve these ends the WTO will:

● provide a "forum" for further trade liberalisation negotiations arising from the Multilateral and Plurilateral Agreements;

● administer the new Dispute Settlement Procedure in such a manner as to regulate and ensure Members' compliance with the agreements;

● establish and direct a Trade Policy Review Mechanism to study the trade policies of Members;

● co-operate fully, and on an equal footing, with the International Monetary Fund and the World Bank for the furtherance of economic policy-making; and

● research and produce both specialised and general economic reports of international interest.

B.4 *Basics*

The WTO is situated at:

> Centre William Rappard
> 154 rue de Lausanne
> 1211 Geneva 21
> Switzerland
>
> Central telephone number: + 41 22 739 5111
> Central fax number: + 41 22 731 4206
> Telex: 41 2 324 GATT CH
> Telegram: GATT, Genève

Companies can obtain information and advice about various trade matters by contacting the General Information and Media Relations Divisions (see below for contact details). For example, many companies have already contacted the Secretariat seeking clarification on the nature and scale of tariff reductions agreed during the Uruguay Round. The WTO provides such information free of charge.

The Director of the General Information and Media Relations Division and WTO spokesman is Keith Rockwell. Contact details for the Division are as follows:

General telephone numbers:	+ 41 22 739 5007
	+ 41 22 739 5019
Fax number:	+ 41 22 739 5458
Information Officer:	+ 41 22 739 5286
	+ 41 22 739 53 93

All enquiries relating to the WTO should be directed to the General Information and Media Relations Divisions. They will either answer queries direct or put the caller in touch with the relevant Secretariat Division (see Table F for structure and divisions of the Secretariat).

The address site of the WTO's website on the internet is:
                    http://www.wto.org
In addition to providing the Centre William Rappard (formerly the GATT acting - headquarters) the Swiss government has also

announced plans to construct additional centres for the WTO, including a "Universal House" for delegates from the developing countries.

All Member's delegates receive diplomatic status in Geneva and are exempt from paying VAT. Spouses of delegates may be granted work permits. There are no WTO branch offices outside of Geneva.

B.5   Structure of the WTO

A diagram detailing the structure of the WTO in full is set out in Table E opposite.
See also Annex 3 for a list of the Chairperson of the WTO's Councils, Committees and Working Parties.

B.5.1   Ministerial Conference

The Ministerial Conference is the top tier of the WTO framework. It is scheduled to meet every two years, with the first meeting due in Singapore, in December 1996.

The Ministerial Conference consists of a representative from each Member and has full authority to take decisions on any matter arising from the Multilateral Trade Agreements. It is the chief policy-making body of the WTO and any major policy changes, such as a decision to alter competition policy or to rewrite the WTO Agreement, require its approval.

B.5.2   General Council

The General Council is responsible for overseeing the WTO between Ministerial Conference meetings and consists of a representative from each Member.

It has authority to act in all areas pertaining to the Multilateral and Plurilateral Trade Agreements and the WTO, save for the making of major policy changes or decisions to alter the WTO constitution. Where Ministerial Conference approval is required, the General Council is not free to initiate discussion for change and carry out all the necessary preparatory work but if no such approval is necessary the General Council can initiate discussion and do preparatory work.

The principle functions of the General Council are:

- to act as a Dispute Settlement Body under the terms of the Understanding on Rules and Procedures Governing the Settlement of Disputes (see section B.14);

- to administer the Trade Policy Review Mechanism (TPRM") (see section B.16); and

- to supervise and ensure the smooth running of the Councils for Trade in Goods, Services and Trade-Related Aspects of Intellectual Property Rights as well as all Trade Committees, including those established under the Ministerial Conference (see sections B.5.3 and B.5.4).

The General Council is designated to meet "as appropriate" but, in practice, this means once every six to eight weeks. Members can choose who they wish to represent them but generally, for most countries, the representatives are the ambassadors (for smaller and/or developing Members) and first secretaries or heads of mission (for these Members which maintain a permanent diplomatic representation mission for WTO matters in Geneva). Where important decisions need to be made, it is normal practice for ambassadors to be requested to attend. It is customary for larger Members to have a specific ambassador to the WTO. A list of Embassies and Ambassadors is contained in Annex 4).

For the day-to-day running of the WTO, the General Council delegates responsibility to three major bodies:

- the Council for Trade in Goods;

- the Council for Trade in Services; and

- the Council for Trade-Related Aspects of Intellectual Property Rights.

These Councils, in turn, oversee various Committees relating to their own particular sector of the Uruguay Round Multilateral Trade Agreements.

The General Council, however, retains overall responsibility for the above-mentioned Councils and their Committees, as well as for the four Committees "established" by the Ministerial Conference and the Committees arising out of the Plurilateral Trade Agreements. It has the authority to vary the procedures of the Trade Councils mentioned above and, if necessary, to replace the Chairmen of both the Councils and Committees. It should be borne in mind that all such decisions of the General Council are made by consensus.

Where a decision cannot be arrived at by consensus, the matter at issue is decided by a vote. Each Member has one vote. The decision is taken in accordance with the majority of votes cast.

In addition to its supervisory role, the General Council can take new work upon itself, for example by making a decision to undertake a study where there has been an implementation problem or by setting up a Working Party (see below) to report on a particular topic. Furthermore, the General Council can ask the Trade Councils (or the Trade Committees directly) to consider and report on a topic normally outside their remit.

As mentioned above, in addition to the Councils, Working Parties can be established by the General Council in order to deal with specific issues defined by the General Council. They are composed of representatives from each Member of the WTO.

A Working Party investigates the matter in question using such sources of expert advice, including the Secretariat, as it so wishes. Having completed its research, the Working Party then draws up a report on the subject and calls a Heads of Delegation meeting.

The Heads of Delegation then meet twice. The first meeting is informal, its purpose being to reach agreement on the findings of the report. The second, formal, meeting then officially proposes that the report go forward to the General Council. In this way, consensus is achieved in advance of the General Council meeting, and the General Council can effectively rubber-stamp the Working Party's findings without additional debate. Where the Working Party concludes that a policy change is required, or some other act requiring approval by the Ministerial Conference, the fact that consensus has already been agreed improves the chances of the Ministerial Conference carrying through that change.

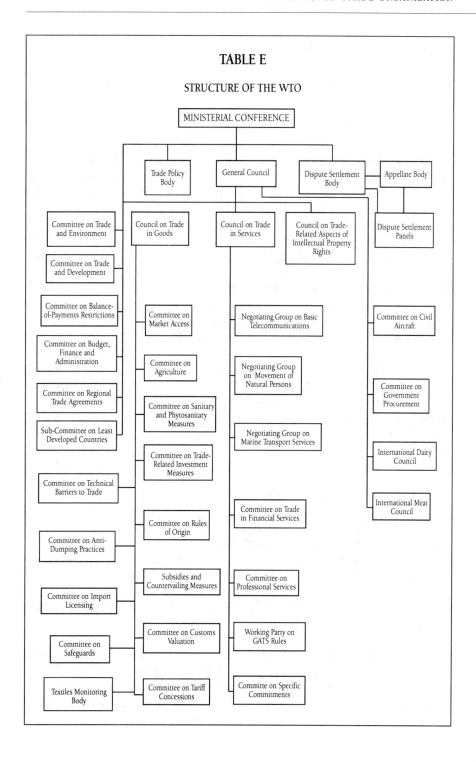

TABLE E

STRUCTURE OF THE WTO

B.5.3 Trade Councils

Every Member is entitled to one vote on each Trade Council.

B.5.3.1 *Council for Trade in Goods*

The Council for Trade in Goods has day-to-day responsibility for over-seeing the proper functioning of all the Multilateral Agreements affecting trade in goods including interpretations of various GATT 1994 articles, (so-called "Understandings") which are found at the beginning of the Uruguay Round Final Act.

At present, the Council for Trade in Goods has responsibility for the Committees on Market Access, Agriculture, Sanitary and Phytosanitary Measures, TRIMS, Rules of Origin, Subsidies and Countervailing Measures, Customs Valuation, Technical Barriers to Trade, Anti-Dumping Practices, Import Licensing, Safeguards, Tariff Concessions and the Textile Monitoring Body.

A point of interest, and perhaps an indication of the future standing of the Trade Councils and the Council for Trade in Goods in particular, is the fact that the Japanese government elected to notify the Council, in addition to the General Council, of its decision to complain against the US's threat to impose tariffs on imported Japanese cars, in April 1995.

B.5.3.2 *Council for Trade in Services*

The Council for Trade in Services is responsible for overseeing (GATS) (see section A.2.13). As indicated above, that agreement consists of a framework of general rules and disciplines for trade in services, together with annexes concerning certain individual services sectors (including Air Transport Services, Financial Services and Telecommunications) and the national schedules of market access commitments made by WTO Members.

At present the Council for Trade in Services has established the Group on Basic Telecommunications, the Negotiating Group on Maritime Transport Services, the Committee on Trade in Financial Services, the Working Party on Professional Services, the Working Party on GATS rules and the Committee on Specific Commitments.

B.5.3.3 *Council for Trade-Related Aspects of Intellectual Property Rights*

The Council for TRIPS manages the operation of the TRIPS Agreement (see section A.2.14), an agreement which includes clauses ensuring non-discrimination, and most-favoured national status, as well as covering different kinds of intellectual property rights such as copyright, trademarks, geographical indications and patents.

The Council for TRIPS has not, to date, established any subsidiary Committees.

B.5.4 Trade Committees

The Trade Committees form the third and final tier of the WTO structure. There are four ways in which they can be established, namely:

- under the terms of one of the Multilateral Trade Agreements (ie the Agriculture Agreement establishes the Committee on Agriculture);

- by one of the Trade Councils, to supervise an area of trade not the subject of its own agreement (ie the Committee for Market Access);

- by the Ministerial Conference; and

- under the terms of one of the Plurilateral Trade Agreements.

The Committees that are established using the first two mechanisms report on their activities to their supervising Trade Council, whereas those established under the second two report directly to the General Council.

Every Member is entitled to one representative on each Trade Committee (with the exception of the Textile Monitoring Body).

General Responsibilities

The Committees are responsible for overseeing the implementation of their specific Multilateral (or Plurilateral) Trade Agreement and/or such designated area of responsibility as decided by the General Council/Trade Councils or as stated in the WTO Agreement.

Each Committee organises its own work procedures (subject to approval of its supervisory body) and may establish further subsidiary Committees if it sees fit.

In addition to supervising an area of trade, the Committees are used as a forum for discussion on ways to improve trade. Furthermore, the General Council and, where relevant, the Trade Councils, can require that a Committee discuss and/or report on a particular matter, even where that matter does not fall within a Committee's normal remit. On average, Committees meet once every two to three months.

Clarifying the status of the Ministerial Conference Committees

The fact that four Committees — Trade and Environment; Trade and Development; Balance of Payment Restrictions; and Budget, Finance and Administration — "shall (according to the WTO Agreement), be established" by the Ministerial Conference, can appear somewhat confusing, particularly when one considers that the Committees are up and running.

The four Committees were established ex-post GATT, by the meeting of Ministers who gathered in Marrakesh in April 1994 to seal the Uruguay Round Agreement. The Committees will be supervised by the General Council; presenting a report there on its first two years of activity.

Individual Committee Responsibilities

The information available on individual Committees varies considerably. For example, the functions and manner of operation of a Committee such as the Textile Monitoring Body are laid down in detail in the Textiles and Clothing Agreement, whilst the TRIMS Agreement gives only general information about the nature of the Committee on TRIMS. The difference becomes even more pronounced where a Committee has been established by the Ministerial Conference or by a Trade Council and is not mentioned in any of the Multilateral Trade Agreements. Unfortunately, the lack of transparency at the WTO (see section C.1) means that little detailed information, outside that printed as part of the Uruguay Round results, is available on the precise workings of the Committees. The sole exception to this is the Committee on Trade and Environment, which has elected to publish a regular newsletter on its activities.

Using all available information, a brief summary of the principal functions and responsibilities of the individual Trade Committees currently in existence is set out below.

B.5.4.1 *Committee on Agriculture*

The Committee on Agriculture is charged with overseeing the successful implementation of the Agriculture Agreement (see section A.2.1). To undertake this, the Committee must request from Members, or request and/or commission from the agriculture division of the Secretariat, such information as it feels necessary in order to carry out a rolling review of the agreement in operation.

The review process will also provide Members with the opportunity to discuss their current and future agricultural reform commitments.

In addition to discussions arising from the review process, Members are required to meet at least once a year for a more general discussion about the growth in world trade in agricultural products (within the confines of commitments already made by them on the limitation of export subsidies). A notification procedure is to operate, whereby any Member that is planning to introduce, or has introduced, a new domestic support measure must inform the Committee and send a copy of the measure in question.

Disputes between Members arising from alleged breaches of the Agriculture Agreement which are not resolved by a Committee's intervention should be referred to the Dispute Settlement Body (see Section B.14.1).

B.5.4.2 *Committee on Sanitary and Phytosanitary Measures*

The Committee on Sanitary and Phytosanitary Measures is responsible for overseeing compliance with the Sanitary and Phytosanitary Agreement (see section A.2.2). As part of this function, the Committee will act as a forum to exchange information on all aspects relating to the implementation of sanitary and phytosanitary measures.

Secondly, the Committee will also seek to encourage the use and/or establishment of international standards by all the Members and will itself sponsor technical reports designed to improve co-ordination between national and international systems for approving the use of food additives or for establishing tolerances for contamination in foods, beverages or animal foodstuffs.

Thirdly, the Committee will maintain close contact with international sanitary and phytosanitary organisations, particularly the Codex Alimentarius Commission, the International Committee of Epizootics and the Secretariat of the International Plant Protection Convention, in order to ensure that it receives the best scientific and technical advice possible to assist with implementing the agreement.

B.5.4.3 *Textiles Monitoring Body*

The Textiles Monitoring Body (the "TMB") supervises the implementation of the Clothing and Textiles Agreement (see section A.2.3). This includes examining the fairness of the remaining restrictive measures of Members as well as those measures introduced as a temporary safeguard.

Unlike other Committees, the TMB does not contain a representative from every Member. Instead, it consists of a Chairman and ten members who are appointed by the Members who have been designated by the Council for Trade in Goods to serve on the TMB. Each appointed member will serve on an individual basis. However, because the TMB is an exception to the WTO principle of one Member, one representative, a system of rotation of Members is to be applied to ensure that a fair balance of interests is maintained at all times.

The TMB is to act as a forum for discussion on any matter relating to the operation of the Textiles and Clothing Agreement and will assist the Council for Trade in Goods in preparing a major review of the operation of the agreement at the end of each of its four stages.

The TMB operates an internal conciliatory procedure where a bilateral disagreement occurs between Members concerning the agreement. The procedure requires the TMB to provide "adequate" opportunities for consultations to take place between the parties included in a dispute. Where, however, despite consultations having taken place, no resolution of differences has been achieved, the TMB can, on the request of either party, after having swiftly but thoroughly considered the problem at hand, make recommendations to the Members involved. Before making any recommendations, the TMB must seek the opinion of any other Member who may be directly affected by the dispute. In any event, the TMB should try to conclude its report within 30 days of the request for assistance. Its recommendations must be sent to all parties involved in the matter and to the Council for Trade in Goods.

The recommendations of the TMB should be accepted in full by the Members. However, where a Member finds it difficult to comply with a recommendation, it must provide the TMB with its reasons within one month after receipt of the TMB's recommendations. The TMB will then make further recommendations, but, if these prove unacceptable as well, either party to the dispute can bring the matter before the WTO Dispute Settlement Body for its consideration.

B.5.4.4 Committee on Technical Barriers to Trade

The Committee on Technical Barriers to Trade is responsible for overseeing the implementation of the Agreement on Technical Barriers to Trade (see section A.2.4). Towards achieving this end, the Committee will carry out an annual review to check that the objectives of the agreement are being achieved. In addition, at the end of every third year, the Committee will undertake a major review of all aspects of the agreement, including its transparency. The aim of the major review will be to ensure that a fair and economically viable balance is maintained between the developed and less developed countries with regard to technical standards required for goods. The Committee will forward to the Council for Trade in Goods any proposals for alterations to the Members obligations that it deems necessary to maintain this balance.

With reference to the less developed countries, the Committee has the authority, if there is a consensus, to grant specified time-limited exemptions, in whole or in part, from obligations under the agreement. The granting of exemptions acknowledges the fact that less developed countries may suffer from structural and developmental problems that make it impossible for them to conform to international technical standards and regulations within the same time-scale as developed nations.

On a more general note, the Committee is to act as a forum for discussion on any matter relating to the operation of the agreement and the furtherance of its objectives. Members will assist the Committee by notifying it of all new (or altered) measures introduced by them under the terms of the agreement.

B.5.4.5 *Committee on Trade-Related Investment Measures*

The Committee on TRIMS has responsibility for the monitoring and implementation of the TRIMS Agreement (see section A.2.5). However, unlike most of the other Committees established by a Multilateral Trade Agreement, the Committee on TRIMS has not been given many specific independent powers. Although it is to act as a forum for discussion on all matters relating to TRIMS, all its other responsibilities are to be assigned to it by the Council for Trade in Goods. Furthermore, it is the Council that is to be notified by Members when any alterations to TRIMS are made or, where a less developed Member seeks an extension in the transition period for the elimination of TRIMS that do not conform to the agreement. In addition, the WTO Secretariat, and not the Committee, is to be notified of the publications in which each Member's TRIMS can be found.

B.5.4.6 *Committee on Anti-Dumping Practices*

The Committee on Anti-Dumping Practices will oversee the implementation of the Anti-Dumping Agreement (see section A.2.6), and act as a forum for consultation between the Members on any matter relating to its operation or the furtherance of its objectives. There are two separate ways for disputes to be resolved. There is the domestic regulation route or the issue can go directly to the WTO for mutilateral dispute resolution.

To assist in carrying out its duties, the Committee may solicit useful information from any international source. However, it must notify in advance, and receive the approval of the Members in which the source is based.

Members must, without delay, report all preliminary or final dumping actions taken to the Committee. The Committee will then make this list available to the public via the WTO Secretariat. In addition, Members must submit a twice-yearly report to the Committee covering all anti-dumping actions taken in the previous six months.

Each Member must notify the Committee of its domestic regulations covering the investigation of anti-dumping practices as well as of the authorities who will carry out the investigations.

At least once a year the Committee will carry out a review of the progress made in implementing the agreement, and will then submit a report to the Council for Trade in Goods setting out the developments made.

B.5.4.7 *Committee on Customs Valuation*

The Committee on Customs Valuation will oversee the implementation of the Customs Valuation Agreement, (see section A.2.7) and act as a forum for consultations between the Members on any matter relating to its operation or the furtherance of its objectives.

However, in addition to the main Committee, the Customs Valuation Agreement also refers to the Technical Committee on Customs Valuation. To make a fairly simplistic comparison between the two would be to say that the Technical Committee takes action to ensure the agreement is implemented, whilst the main Committee observes, discusses and reports on these actions. Although the WTO Secretariat may attend Technical Committee meetings, because it is outside the jurisdiction of the WTO, it may only do so as an observer.

In brief, the Technical Committee:

- gives advice to Members on practical solutions to specific technical problems arising from the day-to-day administration of their customs valuation system;

- undertakes report studies on valuation laws, practices and procedures and provides Members with opinions or explanations on any matter concerning the valuation of imported goods for customs purposes;

- reports annually on the status of the technical elements of the agreement; and

- assists in customs valuation disputes by providing the Dispute Settlement Panel (see section B.14) with a report on their technical aspects.

B.5.4.8 Committee on Rules of Origin

The Committee on Rules of Origin has responsibility for furthering the objectives of the Agreement on Rules of Origin (see section A.2.9), and will act as a forum for consultation between the Members on any related matter. It will provide an annual report to the Council for Trade in Goods, covering all aspects of the agreement in practice.

The principal task of the Committee during its first three years of existence will be, however, to set up, supervise and conclude a work programme designed to bring about greater harmonisation of the rules of origin. In this task, it will be assisted by a Technical Committee, operating under the auspices of the Customs Co-operation Council, an international organisation, independent of the WTO. The Technical Committee has its own rules and procedures, with general responsibilities similar to those of the Technical Committee for Customs Valuation (see section B.5.4.7). Because the Technical Committee is outside of the WTO jurisdiction, the WTO Secretariat has observer status only at its meetings.

The Committee will have overall responsibility for the harmonisation programme, with the Technical Committee in support, carrying out the detailed technical research, analysis and report work necessary to achieve the programme's aims.

At the end of the work programme, the Committee will assess the Technical Committee's findings and draft a report of programme results for submission to the Ministerial Conference. The Ministerial Conference will then set down a timetable for their entry into force and will annex the results to the Agreement on Rules of Origin.

B.5.4.9 Committee on Import Licensing

The Committee on Import Licensing is responsible for overseeing the implementation of the Import Licensing Procedures Agreement, (see section A.2.10), and will also act as a forum for Members to discuss any matter relating to the functioning of the agreement or the furtherance of its objectives.

Members must notify the Committee of any new licensing procedures (or alterations to procedures) that they introduce. Furthermore, Members must identify to the Committee which publications contain their national rules governing procedures for the submission of applications, (including eligibility to make applications, the administrative bodies to be approached and the list of products covered).

At least once every two years, the Committee will undertake a review on the practical workings of the agreement, and will report its findings to the Council for Trade in Goods. To assist the Committee in preparing its review, the WTO Secretariat will prepare a report based on the annual questionnaire responses from Members, detailing their import licensing procedures.

B.5.4.10 Committee On Subsidies and Countervailing

The Committee on Subsidies and Countervailing Measures is responsible for overseeing the implementation of the Agreement on Subsidies and Countervailing Measures, (see section A.2.11), and will, in addition, act as a forum for consultations between the Members on any related matters.
The Committee has set up a Permanent Group of Experts (the "PGE"), consisting of five independent persons with a high level of specialised knowledge and experience in the field of subsidies and trade relations. The Committee chooses the experts and replaces one member per year. Where a Dispute Settlement Panel (see section B.14.3) is considering whether or not a subsidy is "prohibited", the PGE may be asked to act as its expert advisor, and its opinion will be accepted as final. The PGE may also be consulted by any Member to provide a confidential opinion on the nature of a proposed subsidy.

The Committee must be notified by Members of the proposed introduction, or alteration, of any subsidy. In respect of countervailing measures adopted against subsidised imports Members must notify the Committee in report form of all preliminary and final actions taken. The reports should be available for inspection at the WTO Secretariat. Members must also submit twice-yearly reports covering all countervailing duty actions taken in the previous six months.

The Committee has particular responsibility for looking after the interests of developing countries and may grant, in certain circumstances, an extension to the eight year period available to them for phasing out export subsidies. The Committee should also regularly review the position of developing countries with a view to assisting them in carrying out their commitments under the agreement.

The Committee also has an important role to play where a dispute arises as to whether a subsidy is, or is not, non-actionable. Where a dispute exists between two Members on the nature, or possible misuse of, a non-actionable subsidy the matter will be referred to binding arbitration. However, if the subsidy is found to be non-actionable but may still have a serious adverse effect on the domestic industry of another Member, that Member may request consultations in an attempt to clarify and resolve the issue. If, however, after 60 days, no agreement has been reached, the requesting Member may refer the matter to the Committee. The Committee will review all the facts and evidence and will report on whether it believes that a "serious adverse effect" exists. If "serious adverse effects" are confirmed, the Committee will then recommend that modifications be made to the subsidy. However, if the advice is not followed within six months, the Committee can authorise the requesting Member to take appropriate countervailing measures.

The Committee will carry out an annual review of the agreement in practice and will report on the developments to the Council for Trade in Goods. To assist in preparation of the review the Committee can request information from any source, although it must seek the prior approval of a Member in whose jurisdiction a source of information is located.

B.5.4.11 Committee on Safeguards

The Committee on Safeguards is responsible for overseeing the implementation of the Safeguards Agreement, (see section A.2.12), and will act as a forum for consultations between the Members on related matters. The Committee must in particular:

- advise, at the request of a Member, whether the required procedures have been observed in connection with the introduction of a particular safeguard;

- monitor the phasing out of safeguards, orderly market arrangements and voluntary export restraints;

- review (for a Member taking a safeguard measure) whether proposals to suspend concessions or other obligations are "substantially equivalent" to the alleged injury suffered by imports from another Member; and

- report to the Council for Trade in Goods on its findings in all the above matters.

In addition, the Committee as part of its surveillance function will prepare an annual, factual, report on the operation of the agreement, for submission to the Council for Trade in Goods.

B.5.4.12 Committee Market Access

The Committee took over the activities of the old GATT Committee on Tariff Concessions in January 1995. The Committee is responsible for ensuring that the tariff concessions agreed to by Members during the Uruguay Round are actually being adhered to. Particular attention will be paid to agreements such as the Agricultural Agreement, where tariff measures are being reduced in stages and non-tariff measures are being converted into tariffs.

B.5.4.13 Committee on Trade and Environment

The Committee, established at Marrakesh in April 1994, actually came into operation at the beginning of January 1995. It took over from a GATT Sub-Committee on Trade and Environment.

The role of the new Committee is to study the links between trade and the environment and to investigate and report on such issues as:

- the relationship between provisions of multilateral environmental agreements and those of the WTO;

- the impact of environmental measures on market access, particularly for exports of developing countries;

- packaging, labelling and recycling requirements; and

- the transparency of trade-related environmental measures.

The Committee takes its day-to-day direction from the General Council.

It is the only Committee (established as a result of the Uruguay Round) which publishes a newsletter of its activities. Interested parties can receive this free publication by contacting the WTO Information Department (see section B.4).

B.5.4.14 *Committee on Trade and Development*

The Committee on Trade and Development is charged with co-ordinating work on trade and development issues in the WTO. In particular, the Committee is to review the participation of developing country members in the multilateral trading system.

B.5.4.15 *Committee on Balance-of-Payments Restrictions*

The Committee deals with matters concerning less developed countries and particularly those who require exemptions from the Multilateral Trade Agreements in order to satisfy IMF criteria.

B.5.4.16 *Committee on Budget, Finance and Administration*

The Committee looks after internal WTO affairs (see section B.7).

B.5.4.17 *Services Committee*

The Services Committees report to the Council for Trade in Services and have responsibility for specific service sector negotiations that were left incomplete at the time of signing the General Agreement on Trade in Services in December 1993. In their present format, the Services Committees will, for the rest of the year or so, concentrate on providing a forum for discussion between the Members rather than acting as a supervisory body. The following is a brief description of the various Service Committees.

● Negotiating Group on Basic Telecommunications

The group oversees ongoing negotiations between the Members on the liberalisation of the telecommunications market. The negotiations have been carried over from the Uruguay Round and were expected to be completed by the end of April 1996. However, due to lack of agreement the deadline has been extended to February 1997 (see section C.8.5).

- Negotiating Group on Movement of Natural Persons

Negotiations were to have been completed by the end of June 1995 but are still ongoing (see section C.8.5).

- Negotiating Group on Maritime Transport Services

The group oversees ongoing negotiations between Members, carried over from the Uruguay Round. The negotiations have yet to be concluded (see section C.8.5).

- Committee on Trade in Financial Services

Negotiations within this Committee are also continuing (see section C.8.5).

- Committee on Professional Services

The Committee was established to put into effect the work programme on domestic regulation required under GATS. The aim of the Committee is to try and ensure that measures relating to qualification requirements and procedures, as well as technical standards and licensing requirements, in the area of professional services, do not constitute unnecessary trade barriers. Recently the Committee has been studying ways in which the establishment of guidelines for the mutual recognition of qualifications in the accountancy sector could ensure that licensing requirements are not more burdensome than necessary.

B.5.4.18 Intellectual Property Committees

To date, the Council on Trade-Related Aspects of Intellectual Property Rights ("TRIPS") has not established any subsidiary Committees.

B.5.4.19 Plurilateral Trade Agreements Administration Bodies

There are four Plurilateral Trade Agreements for the Administration Bodies, namely:

- the Committee on Government Procurement;

● the Committee on Civil Aircraft;

● the International Meat Council; and

● the International Dairy Council.

Each committee or council is responsible for overseeing the smooth operation of their related Plurilateral Trade Agreement. The Plurilateral Trade Agreements Administration Bodies report directly to the General Council which, in turn, provides them with a certain amount of guidance and direction.

B.5.4.20 *Problems Concerning Representation*

With the exception of the Textile Monitoring Body, the WTO bodies, from the Ministerial Conference to the Trade Committees, are open to representatives from each Member. Unfortunately, this supposed equality of representation fails somewhat in practice. The wealthier and/or larger Members of the WTO have fully staffed diplomatic missions based in Geneva, usually including an ambassador to the WTO. On the other hand, the smaller and/or less developed Members do not have the resources to sustain such a large representation. The result is that it will often be the same person who officially represents his government on a number of different WTO bodies. This makes it difficult, if not impossible, to actually attend all the meetings and, therefore, diminishes the influence of several Members on the world trade stage.

B.6   *The Secretariat*

The Secretariat of the WTO is responsible for servicing the WTO bodies with respect to negotiations and the implementation of agreements. It carries out all the WTO's administration and this includes organising Council and Committee meetings, as well as taking the minutes. In addition, the Secretariat, through its divisions, carries out research at, either the request of the Councils or Committees or of its own volition.

The Secretariat is headed by a Director-General, chosen by consensus, by the Members. Supposedly an apolitical appointment, the appointment of the first elected Director-General Renato Ruggiero, the former Italian foreign minister, (N.B. Peter Sutherland, the former

Director-General of GATT automatically became the first acting WTO Director-General during the initial inception period of the WTO), was fraught with political in-fighting, an early warning perhaps that the WTO may find it difficult to avoid becoming at least a partial hostage to outside political influences.

Renato Ruggiero will serve a four year term as Director-General. He will liaise with and delegate to four Deputy-Director Generals who, in turn, have responsibility for supervising 19 out of 22 Secretariat Divisions, each headed by their own Director. The four Deputy Director- Generals are:

- Warren Lavorel (United States)
- Jésus Seade (Mexico)
- Anwarul Hoda (India)
- Dr Chulsu Kim (South Korea).

See Table F for a diagrammatic view of the hierarchy and divisional structure of the Secretariat. There are currently 450 employees of the Secretariat, although an increase in numbers is anticipated.

On average, a division employs between five to seven professionals, each an expert in his or her field. The exception to this is the Trade and Policy Review Division, which has fifteen employees. As far as is practical, the staff of the Secretariat is meant to be representational of the composition of Members.

The work of the majority of the Secretariat Divisions is fairly self-explanatory, in that they assist Trade Committees of the same name or carry out internal functions at the WTO made clear by their names. However, it is worth elaborating briefly on the responsibilities of some of the Divisions:-

- Translation and Documentation

  This division includes responsibility for the WTO library. The library contains periodicals, essays, theses, IMF/World Bank reports and all manner of books on trade. The library is open to the public. The three official languages of the WTO are English, Spanish and French.

51

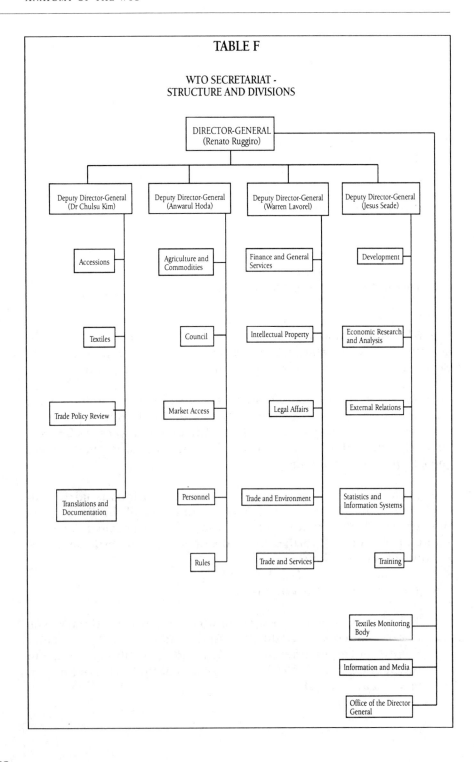

TABLE F

WTO SECRETARIAT -
STRUCTURE AND DIVISIONS

DIRECTOR-GENERAL
(Renato Ruggiro)

Deputy Director-General
(Dr Chulsu Kim)

Deputy Director-General
(Anwarul Hoda)

Deputy Director-General
(Warren Lavorel)

Deputy Director-General
(Jesus Seade)

Accessions

Agriculture and
Commodities

Finance and General
Services

Development

Textiles

Council

Intellectual Property

Economic Research
and Analysis

Trade Policy Review

Market Access

Legal Affairs

External Relations

Translations and
Documentation

Personnel

Trade and Environment

Statistics and
Information Systems

Rules

Trade and Services

Training

Textiles Monitoring
Body

Information and Media

Office of the Director
General

- Legal Affairs

  The division provides legal advice on trade matters relating to the operation of the Trade Agreements. It services the Dispute Settlement Body, provides legal advice to all dispute panels and maintains a dispute settlement data base (ie a legal index for all dispute decisions).

- Rules

  The division services the Anti-Dumping, Safeguards, and Subsidies and Countervailing Measures Committees as well as matters to do with state trading enterprises and trade in civil aircraft.

- Development

  This division liaises with the less developed countries, monitoring regional trading agreements, the operation and implementation of preferential trading regimes applicable between developed and developing countries pursuant to the enabling clause of GATT, the general systems of preferences and schemes such as the EU's Lomé Convention.

- External Relations

  The division liaises with inter-governmental and non-governmental organisations, including handling relations with the OECD and the International Trade Centre, (jointly funded by the WTO and the United Nations Conference on Trade Development ("UNCTAD")).

- Technical Co-operation

  The division assists the developing countries in understanding their commitments to the Multilateral Trade Agreements and to the WTO itself.

B.7 *WTO Budget and Contributions*

The Director-General presents his annual budget estimate and financial statement to the Committee on Budget, Finance and Administration (see section B.5.4.16). The Committee, formed with representatives from each Member, reviews the estimate and makes its recommendations to the General Council. In addition, the Committee proposes the following to the General Council (based on GATT 1947 practices):

- the scale of contributions/apportionment of expenses that should apply between the Members (based on the percentage share of each Member in the total of inter-Member trade); and

- the measures that should be taken against those Members that are in arrears.

The General Council adopts the proposals, and the annual budget estimate, by a two-thirds majority comprising more than half of the Members of the WTO. This is an example of one of the relatively few occasions that the WTO makes a decision based on a vote rather than on consensus.

The current WTO budget is around US$83 million, a sum felt by many, particularly the Director-General and the Secretariat, to be considerably less than is required to ensure the proper functioning of the WTO. WTO officials are paid on average, one third less than their colleagues at the supposedly equally ranked World Bank and IMF.

B.8 *Decision-Making in the WTO*

Decisions of the Ministerial Council, General Council, Trade Councils, and Committees are generally taken by consensus. Consensus is deemed to have been achieved if the chairman of a meeting concludes that no formal objection has been raised against a proposed decision.

Where the Dispute Settlement Body is concerned (see section B.14.1), a reversed consensus approach is applied (ie a consensus is required to halt proceedings or reject related proposals or the adoption of reports).

If no agreement can be reached on a matter requiring a decision, then recourse to voting is provided on the basis of "one country, one vote". Voting margins required are as follows:

- decisions on the interpretation of the provisions of the Trade Agreements require approval by three-quarters of the Members;

- waivers, (ie authorisation in exceptional cases of exemptions for a limited period, from otherwise applicable obligations) also require approval by three-quarters of the Members;

- amendments require the approval of two-thirds of Members provided they "do not change the rights and obligations of Members", with consensus required in other cases; and

- all other decisions are taken by a majority of votes cast.

B.9   *Amendment to Agreements*

Any Member can initiate a proposal to amend the provisions of the WTO Agreement, or the Multilateral Trade Agreements, by submitting such a proposal to the Ministerial Conference. The Councils for Trade in Goods/Services and TRIPS can also submit proposals to the Ministerial Conference, to amend provisions of the Multilateral Trade Agreement which they oversee.

Once an amendment proposal has been made to the Ministerial Conference, a decision has to be made on whether to submit the proposal to the Members for acceptance. If at all possible, that decision should be made by consensus and a period of 90 days, longer if the Ministerial Conference so decides, is allocated for this purpose. If consensus is reached then the Ministerial Conference will immediately submit the proposed amendment to the Members for acceptance. However, if no consensus is reached at the Ministerial Conference within the set period of time, the Conference decides by a two-thirds majority vote whether or not to submit the proposed amendment to the Members for acceptance.

Amendments to the Multilateral Goods Agreements, as well as to GATS and TRIPS, will take effect upon their acceptance by two-thirds of Members — subject to certain exceptions. The exceptions, namely any alteration to MFN treatment or to the WTO decision-making regulations, require acceptance by all the Members. Amendments to the TRIPS agreement which merely serve to increase IPR protection already in force under other agreements, can be adopted by the Ministerial Conference.

B.10 *Founder Members of the WTO*

The founder members of the WTO consisted of 76 out of the 125 GATT contracting parties, including the EU, United States and Japan, who, by 1 January 1995, had accepted the WTO Agreement and the Multilateral Trade Agreements.

For a list of current Members, those in the process of joining and those GATT members who have yet to apply to join, see Annex 2.

B.11 *The Co-existence of GATT and the WTO*

When the Uruguay Round was finally approved in Marrakesh in April 1994 it was clear that not all GATT contracting parties would be able to satisfy the terms for accession to the WTO before it came into force. It was, therefore, thought to be in the interests of the stability of multilateral trade relations that GATT and the WTO continue to co-exist for a period of one year after the WTO's creation.

B.12 *Accession to the WTO*

Any sovereign nation can apply to join the WTO, on terms to be agreed between it and the WTO. All decisions on accession to the WTO are to be taken by the Ministerial Conference or General Council. The procedure for a country seeking to accede to the WTO is as follows:

STEP 1
The applicant makes a formal request to the General Council of the WTO stating its desire to become a member.

STEP 2
The General Council debates the matter and establishes a Working Party to examine the application in detail.

STEP 3
The applicant provides the Accessions Division of the Secretariat (which assists the Working Party), with a full dossier of information concerning all its trade and economic policies (the so-called "Trade Memorandum") that may have a bearing on the Multilateral Trade Agreements.

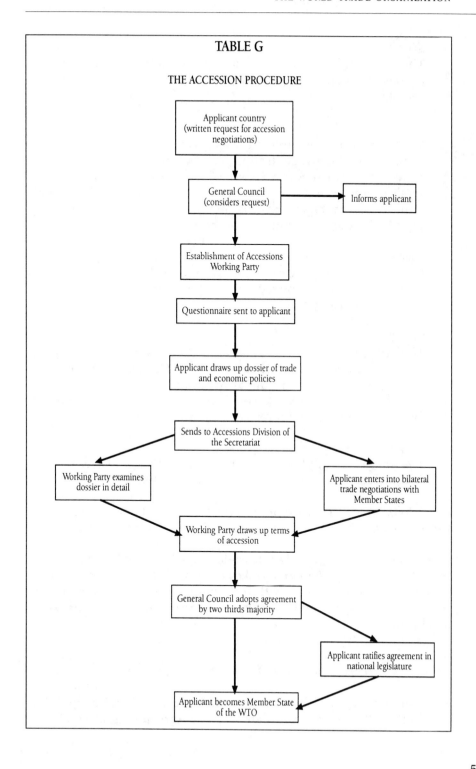

TABLE G

THE ACCESSION PROCEDURE

Applicant country (written request for accession negotiations)

General Council (considers request) → Informs applicant

Establishment of Accessions Working Party

Questionnaire sent to applicant

Applicant draws up dossier of trade and economic policies

Sends to Accessions Division of the Secretariat

Working Party examines dossier in detail

Applicant enters into bilateral trade negotiations with Member States

Working Party draws up terms of accession

General Council adopts agreement by two thirds majority

Applicant ratifies agreement in national legislature

Applicant becomes Member State of the WTO

STEP 4

The Working Party carries out a detailed examination of the proposed accession based on the information provided to the Secretariat.

STEP 5

Whilst the Working Party is carrying out its duties, the applicant country should engage itself in bilateral negotiations with other Members with a view to achieving a mutually agreed level of concessions and commitments for goods (and services). The negotiating process enables existing Members to judge the benefit of permitting the applicant to join the WTO.

STEP 6

Once the Working Party examination and the bilateral negotiations have been completed, terms of accession are drawn up by the Working Party.

STEP 7

The Working Party's report, along with a draft accession agreement (including an attached schedule of concessions/commitments) are presented to the Ministerial Conference or General Council for adoption. A two-thirds majority of Members in favour is required to approve accession.

STEP 8

The successful applicant accedes to the WTO, after having ratified the accession agreement in its national legislature.

It should be noted that accessions to the Plurilateral Trade Agreements are governed by the provisions contained in those agreements.

Those countries recognised as "least-developed" by the United Nations are only to be required to undertake commitments and concessions to an extent that is consistent with their individual development, financial and trade needs or with their administrative and institutional capabilities.

B.13 *Withdrawal from the WTO*

Any Member may withdraw from the WTO, such withdrawal applying to both the WTO and the Multilateral Trade Agreements, by sending a formal written notice of withdrawal to the Director-General of the WTO. The actual withdrawal will take place six months after receipt of the notice.

Withdrawal from a Plurilateral Trade Agreement is governed by the provisions of that agreement.

B.14 *WTO Dispute Settlement Mechanism*

According to the Understanding on Rules and Procedures Governing the Settlement of Disputes:

> "the dispute system of the WTO is a central element in providing security and predictability to the multilateral trading system".

The new dispute mechanism is far more detailed than the old GATT procedures, which were contained in just two articles and supplemented by an interpretative document published in 1981. By contrast the WTO procedures run to 27 sections, totalling 143 paragraphs, plus 4 appendices.

Under the new rules, a single Dispute Settlement Body is set up to handle disputes, whereas the GATT dispute settlement body was split between the Council and various Tokyo Round Committees.

Under the new system, there needs to be consensus against the establishment of a dispute settlement panel (a "Disputes Panel") (see below) for a complaint not to progress. This means that the Member which is being complained against can no longer block single-handedly a complaint just because it fears it may lose.

Unlike under the old GATT dispute system, it will now be possible to appeal against a Disputes Panel decision, to a standing Appellate Body (see below). Finally, a prejudiced Member can be authorised to take retaliatory action against an offending Member that has failed to implement an approved panel recommendation within a reasonable period of time.

A flow chart of the dispute settlement procedure can be found in Table H (see also section B.14.6 below).

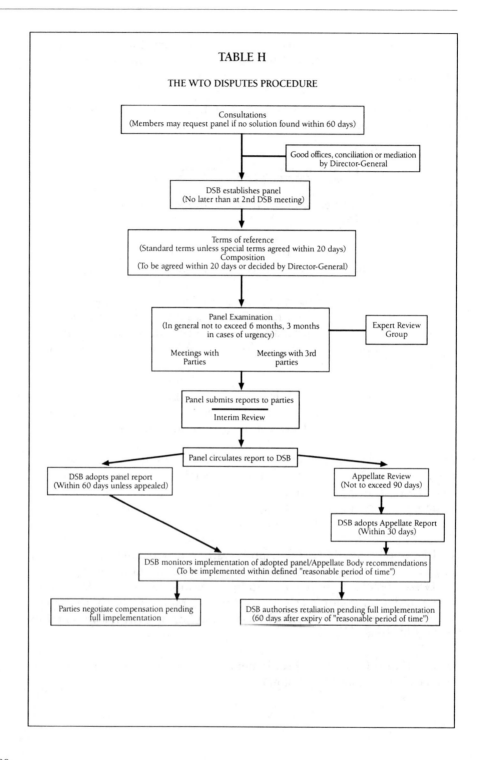

TABLE H

THE WTO DISPUTES PROCEDURE

Consultations
(Members may request panel if no solution found within 60 days)

Good offices, conciliation or mediation
by Director-General

DSB establishes panel
(No later than at 2nd DSB meeting)

Terms of reference
(Standard terms unless special terms agreed within 20 days)
Composition
(To be agreed within 20 days or decided by Director-General)

Panel Examination
(In general not to exceed 6 months, 3 months
in cases of urgency)

Meetings with   Meetings with 3rd
Parties   parties

Expert Review
Group

Panel submits reports to parties

Interim Review

Panel circulates report to DSB

DSB adopts panel report
(Within 60 days unless appealed)

Appellate Review
(Not to exceed 90 days)

DSB adopts Appellate Report
(Within 30 days)

DSB monitors implementation of adopted panel/Appellate Body recommendations
(To be implemented within defined "reasonable period of time")

Parties negotiate compensation pending
full impelementation

DSB authorises retaliation pending full implementation
(60 days after expiry of "reasonable period of time")

B.14.1 The Dispute Settlement Body

The Dispute Settlement Body (the "DSB") is the body that has overall charge of the dispute settlement mechanism. It is in effect the General Council in a different guise, and consists of a representative from each Member. It is the DSB which must ultimately decide whether or not a Member has broken any rules governing the WTO Agreement or one of the Multilateral Trade Agreements. In carrying out this role, the DSB is variously assisted by the good offices of the Director-General, the Disputes Panel and, possibly, the Appellate Body.

Before detailing the procedural aspects of the dispute settlement mechanism, the various component bodies are described first.

B.14.2 The "Good Offices" of the Director-General

The Director-General can be asked to intervene in a dispute between two Members or, as in the USA v. Japan car import dispute, he can remind the parties of their responsibilities to consult and thereafter to follow WTO Disputes Procedure rather than take unilateral action.

In offering his "good offices", the Director-General is likely to offer his personal advice in conjunction with the advice of key advisors from WTO Secretariat, including the head of the legal division. The advice of the Director-General and his assistants is not binding and cannot be cited in a later Disputes Panel report.

B.14.3 Disputes Panel

If a dispute has not been resolved by consultations between the parties, or with the aid of the good offices of the Director-General, it is referred to a Dispute Panel. The Dispute Panel is established by the DSB, and consists of three to five independent panellists, with a "sufficiently diverse background and a wide spectrum of experience".

The sort of background and experience envisaged for a panellist includes government and/or non-government individuals, who have:

- served on some form of a panel in the past or presented a case to a panel; or

- acted as a government representative under GATT, or on a WTO Council or Committee; or

- been employed as an expert by the Secretariat; or

- taught or published on international trade law or policy; or

- served as a senior trade policy official of a Member.

A list of potential panellists, with their qualifications, is maintained by the Secretariat in order to assist with selection. The list will specify the areas and extent of expertise of each individual, with regard to the Trade Agreements. Members will be free to propose new individuals from time to time and, if approved by the DSB, they will be added to the list.

The task of the Disputes Panel is to investigate thoroughly the facts of the dispute, taking into account the terms of the particular agreement alleged to be breached. It must consult with both parties to the dispute in order to gain the fullest understanding possible of the problem and should encourage them to reach a mutually acceptable solution, if at all possible. The Disputes Panel, in undertaking its investigations shall have recourse to such information as it feels will assist in its deliberations including, for matters of a technical nature, the setting up of an Expert Review Group (see below).

Where the two parties to a dispute have failed to reach an acceptable agreement during the investigation, the Disputes Panel will present a written report to the DSB, setting out:

- its findings of fact;

- the applicability of relevant agreement provisions; and

- the reasoning behind its recommendations.

After the settlement of a dispute, the names of the Disputes Panel members, and those of any Expert Review Group employed, will be made available to the public.

B.14.4 Expert Review Group

Where a Disputes Panel is considering a matter of a particularly technical nature it may, with the consent of both parties to the dispute, establish an Expert Review Group ("ERG") to provide it with assistance.

The ERG takes its reference and working procedures from the Disputes Panel and presents it with a written report.

An ERG will consist of experts in the particular field under investigation. They serve as individuals and should not, save for in exceptional circumstances, be citizens of a party to the dispute.

The Secretariat will draw up a list of potential experts although the Disputes Panel itself may suggest potential members. Any expert who is interested in the possibility of becoming a member of an ERG should submit his or her name and details to the WTO Secretariat. As with the Disputes Panel, an ERG may seek information and technical advice from any source and Members should respond promptly to any questions put to them.

Both sides to the dispute will have access to the ERG's information unless it is of a confidential nature in which case it may not be released without the permission of the government or organisation providing it. Where confidential information is passed to the ERG but permission is not granted for its publication, the government or organisation involved will formulate a non-confidential summary for distribution to the parties.

The ERG will initially produce a draft report and submit it to both parties to the dispute for their comments. These comments should be taken into account when producing the final report, a copy of which will go to both parties at the same time as it is presented to the Disputes Panel. The ERG's report is of an advisory nature only, although it will obviously carry not inconsiderable weight when it comes to the Dispute Panel presenting its overall findings to the DSB.

B.14.5 The Appellate Body

Where a party to a dispute disagrees with a Disputes Panel recommendation, it can appeal to a standing Appellate Body, established by the DSB. The appeal, however, is limited to issues of law covered in the Disputes Panel report and the legal interpretation developed by the Disputes Panel.

The Appellate Body is composed of seven people who will serve for a four year term (with one possible extension of four years). Only three of the seven will serve on any one case and, to ensure an even distribution of work, the members will serve in rotation. The current members are: James Bacchus (United States), Christopher Beeby (New Zealand), Professor Claus-Dieter Ehlermann (Germany), Dr Said El-Naggar (Egypt), Justice Florentino Feliciano (Philippines), Julio Lacarte Muro (Uruguay) and Professor Mitsuo Matsushita (Japan).

The Appellate Body representatives must be people of recognised standing in the field of law and international trade and not be affiliated to any government. They are appointed on the basis of a joint proposal forwarded by the Director-General, the DSB Chairman and the Chairmen of the General Council and the Trade Councils. The representatives, who must be available at short notice, will receive a monthly retainer plus travel expenses and allowances when they are required to be in Geneva. There is, in addition, a support staff consisting of a registrar, three professional assistants and clerical staff. The support staff will be employed by the WTO but will be separate from the Secretariat and will be answerable to the Appellate Body. When an appeal comes before the Appellate Body for its consideration, its proceedings will be confidential, based on information already provided in the dispute and without the presence of either party. After having reviewed the evidence, the Appellate Body reports to the DSB. Its findings must be accepted by the parties to the dispute unless the DSB decides, by consensus, not to adopt the report. The Appellate Body can decide to uphold, modify or reverse the legal findings and conclusions of the Disputes Panel.

B.14.6 The WTO Disputes Procedure

See also Table H.

STEP 1
Where a dispute arises between two or more Members concerning the alleged breach by a Member of its obligations under the Trade Agreements or the WTO Agreement, the aggrieved Member should make a request for consultations with the offending Member. The request must be sent to the DSB in writing, setting out the reasons behind its submission, including an identification of the measure in issue and the legal basis for the complaint.

STEP 2

A reply should be made by the complained against Member within 10 days (unless otherwise mutually agreed) and consultations should commence within 30 days of the original request. Where a case is urgent or involves perishable goods the reply and commencement of consultations should take place within 10 days of the original request.

STEP 3

Where consultations fail and where both parties agree the case can be brought before the Director-General who, acting in an ex-officio capacity, will be ready to offer his "good offices", conciliation or mediation (see section B.14.2) to settle the dispute.

It should be noted that the good offices procedure may continue while the Disputes Panel process is in progress, provided both parties agree to it.

STEP 4

If no response to a request for consultations is received within 10 days or, if the consultations fail to achieve a solution after 60 days, the complainant can ask the DSB to establish a Disputes Panel (see section B.14.3) to examine the case.

The establishment of a Disputes Panel is almost automatic since the DSB must undertake this step no later than the second time it considers the panel request, unless there is a consensus against forming it. The negative consensus requirement is one that makes it very difficult for a Member which is subject to a complaint to halt its progress.

STEP 5

A Disputes Panel is to be constituted within 20 days of the DSB's decision to establish it. Its terms of reference — which are laid out in the Understanding on Rules and Procedures Governing the Settlement of Disputes — mandate it to examine the complaint in the light of the particular agreement cited and to present findings that will assist the DSB in making recommendations or in giving rulings required by the agreement. Different terms of reference may be employed if both parties to the dispute agree within 20 days of the establishment of the Disputes Panel.

Where the parties to the dispute cannot agree, within 20 days, on the panellists nominated by the Secretariat, the Director-General in conjunction with the Chairman of the relevant Council/Committee, will decide the appointments.

STEP 6

From the time that the Disputes Panel's terms of reference and composition are agreed it should, within six months, aim to complete its examination of the case and produce a final report (three months for urgent cases such as those relating to perishable goods) and, should never take more than nine months.

The Disputes Panel should meet with both parties to the dispute at least twice and has the authority to seek information and assistance from any source. It may, if it deems it necessary, establish an Expert Review Group (see section B.14.4) to prepare a report on a technical matter beyond its own range of expertise.

It is the Disputes Panel's duty to make an objective assessment of the case before it and it should continue, throughout the course of its investigations, to encourage the parties to the dispute to settle the matter voluntarily.

STEP 7

After the Disputes Panel has considered the written and oral evidence of both parties to the dispute it will distribute the factual and argument sections of its report to the parties for their perusal. The parties will then submit their written comments within a prescribed time period set by the panel.

STEP 8

Following receipt of both parties comments on the descriptive sections of the report the Disputes Panel will issue an interim report to the parties of its findings and conclusions. It will set a period of time in which the parties can respond to the interim report and this may include a further meeting to discuss any written comments made. Where no comments are made on the interim report, it will be considered as the final report.

STEP 9

The final report is submitted to the DSB who should adopt it within 60 days of issuance unless either one of the parties to the dispute indicates that it intends to appeal or a consensus emerges in the DSB against adoption.

Before the DSB can consider adopting the report, it must first circulate it to the other Members. Members who object to the report then have the opportunity to write to the DSB outlining those objections at least 10 days before the meeting at which the Disputes Panel report is due to be discussed. For this reason, the DSB has to wait at least 20 days after circulating the report to Members, before holding an adoption meeting.

STEP 10

Provided that no appeal has been lodged against the Disputes Panel report and that there is no consensus against adoption the DSB will automatically approve the panel's recommendations at the adoption meeting.

STEP 11

Either party to the dispute may appeal against the final report, to the standing Appellate Body (see section B.14.5), which will be restricted to issues of law covered in the report and legal interpretations developed by the Disputes Panel. The Appellate Body will review the existing evidence and should aim to report to the DSB with its findings within 60 days (and certainly never more than 90 days).

STEP 12

The DSB must adopt the Appellate Body report within 30 days of issuance, unless there is consensus against adoption. At this stage (or after Step 10, if no appeal is lodged) both parties to the dispute are bound to accept, unconditionally, the recommendations of the Appellate Body (or Disputes Panel).

STEP 13

At a DSB meeting to be held within 30 days after the adoption of the Disputes Panel, or Appellate Body report, the party concerned must state its intentions in respect of the implementation of the DSB's recommendations.

STEP 14

The DSB will allow the concerned party a "reasonable period of time" to implement the recommendations. In any event that reasonable period should not normally exceed 15 months from the report's original date of adoption.

67

STEP 15

In the event that a party fails to comply with the recommendations within the set time, it must enter into negotiations with the
complainant in order to decide on a mutually acceptable level of
compensation.

STEP 16

If, after 20 days of the expiry of the "reasonable time" no acceptable level of compensation has been agreed, the complainant
may request authorisation from the DSB to suspend concessions
or obligations due to the offending party under the particular
agreement in question (but see this section below).

STEP 17

The DSB should grant the request for suspension of concessions
or obligations, within 30 days of the expiry of the reasonable
time, unless there is a consensus against doing so.

STEP 18

If the offending party objects to the level of suspension granted
by the DSB, it can request that the matter be sent to arbitration.
Arbitration should be carried out by the original Disputes
Panel's members or, if this proves impossible, by an arbitrator
appointed by the Director-General. The arbitration process
should be completed within 60 days of the expiry of the "reasonable time" and its decision is final.

STEP 19

On request from the complainant, the DSB will then authorise
the suspension of concessions as recommended by the arbitration board, unless there is a consensus against so doing.

In principle, the DSB (or arbitration body) should authorise (or
recommend), the suspension of concessions, in the same sector
of an agreement. However, if this is not practicable or does not
produce the desired effect, authorisation may be granted to suspend concessions in a different sector of the same agreement or,
where the circumstances are serious enough, under another
agreement. In general terms, withdrawal of concessions will take
the form of increased import duties.

The object of the extensive series of sanction possibilities is to
make life as difficult as possible for a Member that breaks its

promises towards the Trade Agreements or the WTO itself, and so to actively dissuade such activity. Nevertheless, it must be borne in mind that the WTO has no legal powers to force a Member to uphold their obligations by means, for example, of a direct fine. Ultimately, the WTO's enforcement powers rest in persuasion and in the moral force of its argument, or the strength of the Member adopting retaliatory action.

B.14.6.1 *Third Parties to a Dispute*

At the consultations stage, a third party Member that believes it has a substantial trade interest in the dispute may notify the DSB and the main parties of its desire to be joined in the talks. This notification must be made within 10 days of the original request for consultations. It is up to the Member to whom the original request for consultations was made, to decide whether the third party has a sufficient trade interest.

At the Disputes Panel stage, a third party who has notified the DSB of a substantial interest in the ongoing dispute will be granted permission to make written and oral submissions to the panel. The submissions will be taken into account in the final report. In addition to making submissions, an interested third party will receive copies of the submissions made by the main parties to the dispute to the first Disputes Panel meeting.

Where a third party concludes that a trade measure which is the subject of current proceedings, has a negative effect on benefits accruing to it under any agreements it may have recourse to the Disputes Procedure. However, in such circumstances, the dispute will be referred to the original Disputes Panel, if at all possible.

B.14.6.2 *Multiple Complaints*

If more than one Member requests the establishment of a Disputes Panel on the same matter a single Disputes Panel will be set up to consider all the complaints, whenever possible.

Each complainant will have the right to be present at the oral submissions of the other, and to receive copies of written submissions.

If one of the complainants so requests, the Disputes Panel will present separate reports at the completion of its investigations.

In the event that a multiple complaint is heard by more than one panel, wherever possible the same panellists should serve on the separate panels, with the timetable for the panel process harmonised.

B.14.6.3 *The Dispute Mechanism in Practice*

The first dispute lodged under the WTO dispute settlement mechanism was a complaint made by Singapore against Malaysia, concerning the latter's restrictions on imports of polyethylene and polypropylene. The dispute was settled at the consultations stage after Malaysia decided to modify the offending measure by making the applicable licensing system automatic.

The first dispute to reach the Disputes Panel stage was a complaint made by Venezuela against the United States, concerning the US Environmental Protection Agency's new standards for reformulated and conventional gasoline. Venezuela claimed that the new standards imposed higher standards for its gasoline than those applied to the US domestic market and some other countries. The complaint was based on a violation of Articles III and I of GATT 1995 (national treatment and Most Favoured Nation status), as well as a breach of the Agreement on Technical Barriers to Trade (the creation of unnecessary obstacles to trade). Australia, Canada, the EU and Norway participated in the proceedings as third parties. The Disputes Panel ultimately ruled in favour of Venezuela. An appeal launched in favour of the United States was unsuccessful.

For a full list of complaints referred to the dispute settlement mechanism during the first six months of its existence, see Annex 1.

B.15 *WTO Relationship with the IMF and World Bank*

The WTO officially has equal international status with the IMF and the World Bank. One of its principal functions, as stated in the WTO Agreement, is to cooperate with both the above institutions "with a view to achieving greater coherence in global economic policy-making". Indeed, to further reinforce this aim, a separate Ministerial Declaration was made at Marrakesh in April 1994.

The actual development of relations between the WTO and its counterparts remains the responsibility of the Director-General. It is for him to develop a coherent and effective strategy. However, there is still no certainty as to what form that co-operation would take or how it would evolve.

What is certain is that a close relationship between the WTO, IMF and World Bank is imperative if the participation of less developed countries in the move towards increased liberalisation of world trade is to be maintained. Without these countries' full participation, the results of the Uruguay Round will be greatly diminished. However, they need to be able to participate and this requires the formulation of a good economic policy that both takes into account the particular problems they face, and makes a serious attempt to address them.

B.16 *The Trade Policy Review Mechanism*

The Trade Policy Review Mechanism (the "TPRM") is a function of the WTO whose purpose is to monitor the trade policies and practices of the Members and to assess their impact on the multilateral (and, where relevant, plurilateral) trading system. The objective of the review is to achieve a greater degree of transparency and understanding of these policies and thus to assist towards a smoother running of the trade system.

The TPRM is carried out under the auspices of the Trade Policy Review Body — a manifestation of the General Council of the WTO (see WTO Structure set out in Table E). It undertakes to carry out a periodic review of the trade policies of Members, the frequency of the review being dependent on the share of world trade attributable to each of them. The largest four trading Members, including the EU, will be subject to a review every two years. The next sixteen largest Members will face a review every four years, with other Members being reviewed every six years, apart from the least developed Members, for whom a longer period may be agreed.

In order to assist the Review Body between reviews and to further improve transparency Members will provide a brief annual update of statistical trade information along with details of any major policy changes. Special consideration will be given to the difficulties involved in the less developed countries providing such information, with technical assistance being made available by the Secretariat where requested.

Where a major review is being carried out, the Review Body will base its work on:

● a full report of trade policies and practices supplied by the Members (including material from annual up-date reports); and

● a report prepared by the Secretariat based on information it has acquired and/or which has been provided by the Members. The Secretariat should seek clarification of stated Member trade policies and practices when preparing its report.

Both reports will be considered at a Review Body meeting and will, along with the minutes of the meeting, be published shortly thereafter. A copy of the reports and Review Body minutes will also be passed on to the Ministerial Conference for its information.

In addition to carrying out regular reviews of the WTO membership, the Review Body will also prepare an annual overview of those developments in international trade which are causing an impact on the multilateral trading system. It will be assisted in this by receiving an annual report prepared by the Director-General, highlighting those policy issues which are having an effect on trade.

At the end of the first five years of operation of the TPRM, the Review Body will carry out an appraisal of how well the review process has worked. The results of its appraisal will be presented to the Ministerial Conference for its consideration.

B.17 *The European Union and the WTO*

Although there are a number of economic interest groupings within the WTO, such as NAFTA (North American Free Trade Area), the Members of ASEAN (Association of South East Asian Nations) and the Cairns Group of agricultural exporting nations, only the EU — a customs union with a single external tariff — is a member of the WTO in its own right, in addition to each of its constituent members.

As both the EU and the EU's Member States are full members of the WTO they are entitled to representation at the Ministerial Conference and, on the General Council, Trade Councils and various Committees. In situations where a vote is required, the EU is entitled to as many votes as it has members who are also members of the WTO, currently 15. In terms of who should represent the EU itself in negotiations within the WTO, that role will largely be carried out by the European Commission ("the Commission"). However, in November 1994, the European Court of Justice ("the ECJ") in a case deliberately brought before it to resolve the issue, ruled that EU Member States had the right to be separately involved in certain multilateral trade negotiations such as trade in services and intellectual property.

A Code of Conduct for WTO Business, was drawn up by the Commission in May 1995 and is currently under discussion. The Code's aim is to ensure that the EU is able to speak as one on issues within the WTO, whilst taking into account the ECJ's judgement.

The Code sets out the following rules of conduct:

- In the defence and negotiation of common positions, the Commission will act on behalf of the EU after having consulted with the Article 113 Committee (which deals with the Common Commercial Policy and contains representatives from both the Commission and EU Member States). In all cases, the Commission will prepare a draft course of action where three or more EU Member States feel that a statement should be made or a specific measure adopted;

- At the Ministerial Conference, Ministers of EU Member States can speak on any matters, including those relating to the budget or administration of the WTO. However, their comments should be in line with general EU policy;

- At all plenary meetings both the Commission and the EU Member States will maintain a full presence. However, if a restricted meeting is held within the WTO framework, attendance should be limited to the Commission and the then current president of the EU Council (the presidency of the EU Council rotates every six months amongst the EU's Member States). Nevertheless, if an EU Member State believes that the Commission is straying from a previously agreed position or course of action or, where some other strange turn of events occurs, it can request a halt in the proceedings; and

- In dispute settlements involving the EU, the Commission will act on behalf of the members.

In conclusion, the Commission is to represent the EU on matters relating to trade in goods, whilst the EU Member States retain individual jurisdiction in most areas relating to trade in services and intellectual property.

c. THE WTO AND BUSINESS

C.1 *Transparency and the WTO*

GATT was much criticised for its lack of internal transparency. Almost all GATT documents were listed as being restricted, regardless of content. As recently as October 1994, the US government complained that the balance between the need for confidentiality surrounding the discussions of GATT contracting states and the need for public awareness, was not being achieved. The US government was particularly concerned that, as WTO procedures were to be based on those of GATT, the problem would continue.

Regrettably, the US government's fears have proved well founded. At present, all information relating to discussions and decisions that take place at the Ministerial Conference, General Council, Trade Councils and Committees, is classified as restricted, unless there is a consensus to release material. To date, only one Committee, that on Trade and the Environment, has elected to release material in the form of a newsletter outlining its agenda and containing details of its meeting discussions. The transparency of the WTO is, however, under constant review, and the likelihood remains that transparency will gradually improve over a period of time. It is certainly expected that more Committees will produce some form of newsletter covering their activities. The best that can be hoped for in the near future is the planned production of WTO annual reports summarising the activities of all WTO sectors.

C.2 *Educational Courses*

The WTO runs nine-week trade policy courses throughout the year, aimed at government employees from developing countries. The courses are held in English, French or Spanish. Contact the Information and Media Division (see section B.4) for further information.

C.3 *Educational Visits*

Group visits from companies or associations are welcomed by the WTO and can be fixed by prior arrangement with the Information and Media Division (see section B.4). Such a visit could include a tour of the WTO combined with lectures from relevant Secretariat divisions.

C.4 *Publications*

The WTO produces a wide range of publications for sale to the public. These range from general texts on world trade, to specific sectoral analysis reports and political and commercial studies of individual Members. The Economic Research Division can undertake new work either at its own instigation, or at the request of the General Council, Trade Councils or Committees.

In addition to publications for sale, the WTO produces several free publications. The most important of these is the WTO Focus newsletter, which contains an overview of current activities within the WTO and is published six times a year. Anyone can subscribe to the newsletter by contacting the Information and Media Division.
The Trade and Environment Committee's newsletter is also free and, similarly, can be subscribed to as above. There is no set date for its publication as it depends on the frequency of the Committee meetings.

The WTO has an annual booklet that lists all its current publications. For a copy, contact the Information and Media Division.

C.5 *Influencing Policy — Lobbying*

The nature of the WTO means that all discussions are held, and decisions made, at inter-governmental level. It is recommended, therefore, that lobby groups and/or trade associations concentrate the main part of their campaign on seeking to influence the formation of policy at a national level. Lobbying the WTO is more complicated because the representatives of Members cannot make personal decisions on policy matters.

Nevertheless, lobbying at the Trade Committees is permitted and, despite the fact that attendance by the public at Committee meetings is prohibited, a number of lobby groups and trade associations have thought it wise to establish a presence in Geneva. The fact is that if a lobby group can impress sufficient numbers of Member representatives on a particular Committee of the strength of their case, those representatives may recommend a change of policy when they report back to their governments. Their governments may well be more inclined to change their policy if the representative indicates that a majority of other representatives also shared the same positive view of the lobby group's case. At worst, by lobbying the representatives of a Committee, a lobby group will ensure that its point of view reaches an international audience in a short space of time. Lobbying the WTO may, therefore, be a very useful addition to work at a national level.

C.6 *Breach of a Multilateral Trade Agreement — Procedures for Companies*

Where a company, based in Member A believes that as a result of a breach in a Trade Agreement by Member B, it is being prejudiced, what is its course of action?

The WTO deals at an inter-governmental level and, therefore, a company cannot approach it direct with a complaint about the prejudicial behaviour of another Member. What it must do is advise its own government of the breach (in the event that its government is unaware) and attempt to persuade it to lodge a complaint with the WTO. Member A and Member B would then follow the disputes procedure laid down in the Dispute Settlement Mechanism (see section B.14). The EU and the United States have established procedures for such "third party complaints" (see Tables I and J).

C.7 *Legal Remedies for Breach of WTO Law*

According to well-established case law of the ECJ, private parties are not entitled to rely on GATT provisions in proceedings before the courts of EU Member States. In other words, GATT provisions are not capable of producing "direct effect". Thus, with the notable exception of the public procurement code discussed above, individuals and companies may not launch claims before national courts against, for example, acts of the authorities of EU Member States, which infringe against GATT and WTO rules.

TABLE I

Third Party Complaints Procedure in the EU

Under the EU's Trade Barrier Regulation (Regulation 3286/94, OJ L 349/71 31.12.94) the following procedure has been adopted for companies or private individuals who believe they are facing discrimination by a non-EU country which contravenes WTO rules.

* A prospective complainant should informally contact the Commission in order to get an idea of the issues involved and the amount of evidence that will be needed to prove that WTO rules are being breached.

* A complaint is submitted to the Commission in writing. It will then be circulated to the EU's Member States for comments.

* The Commission has 45 days after a formal complaint is received to decide whether it is admissible. This deadline may be suspended at the request of the complainant, in order to allow it to provide further information.

* If the complaint is ruled admissible a formal investigation is initiated by the Commission. The Commission will then hold further discussions with the complainant and interested parties, as well as holding consultations with the third countries concerned and the EU Member States. The investigation may take between five and seven months at the end of which the Commission will submit a report to the Member States of the EU.

* If the Commission considers that it has a good chance of winning a case it will initiate the Dispute Settlement Procedure.

* If, after a successful outcome under the Dispute Settlement Procedure, the country or countries responsible fail to put an end to the practice complained of, and no other solution can be found, the Council may adopt retaliatory measures on the basis of a Commission proposal, within 30 working days.

TABLE J

Third Party Complaints Procedures in the US

Under Title III of the US Trade Act 1974 (known as "Section 301") an individual or private party can petition the United States Trade Representative ("USTR") to instigate the appropriate action under WTO rules.

- An interested party files a petition with the USTR requesting it to take retaliatory action under Section 301

- Within 45 days of receiving the complaint the USTR must determine whether to initiate a Section 301 investigation

- If the USTR initiates a formal investigation it must, on the same day, request consultations with the country or countries against whom the complaint has been made. Consultations with the third country/countries must not take longer than 150 days.

- If initial consultations are unsuccessful the USTR must initiate the WTO Dispute Resolution Procedure. The USTR has a certain amount of discretion in deciding if the actions of a foreign government fall within WTO rules. The USTR must seek information and advice from the complainant, and the appropriate private sector advisory committees, when preparing a submission to the Dispute Settlement Body. The USTR can also hold public hearings and request information from other interested parties.

- The USTR can take action 30 days after the completion of the procedure under the Dispute Settlement Proceeding or 18 months after the initiation of a WTO dispute settlement. If the WTO Dispute Panel finds that there has not been a violation of WTO rules, the USTR can still initiate retaliatory action, even though such action could breach WTO rules.

- The original complainant, or a majority of US industry, or the USTR, can request a 90 or 180 day delay in retaliatory action. During this period the USTR can continue negotiations with the third country or countries involved.

- Once this extension expires, if the third country has not complied with the WTO ruling, the USTR must impose retaliatory action.

- The USTR will continue to monitor the relevant third country/countries' compliance with the WTO ruling. If the country/countries fail to implement the WTO's rulings within a reasonable time the USTR must decide within 30 days of the expiry of this time what retaliatory action it should take.

In justifying its position, the ECJ has not considered the particular terms of specific provisions of GATT. Instead, it has repeatedly pointed out that GATT was founded on the principle of negotiations undertaken on a reciprocal basis and that it is important for its application that there should be a balance of advantages and disadvantages for its members. The GATT provisions are, according to the ECJ, flexible and allow for derogations and for measures to be taken in cases of exceptional difficulty. Also of importance for the ECJ are the methods of dispute settlement, essentially based on consultations and negotiations conducted by the authorities of the EU Members States, with no private party involvement. The Court has also repeatedly held that in the event of a failure of EU Member States to carry out obligations under GATT, GATT allows other EU Member States adversely affected thereby to suspend the application of their own obligations, a concept similar to reprisals under international law rather than enforcement of court judgements.

The case law of the ECJ has been confirmed by an EU Council Decision of 22 December 1994 concerning the conclusion, on behalf of the European Community, of the agreements reached in the Uruguay Round. The last recital of the preamble of this Decision states expressly that the agreement establishing the WTO, including the annexes thereto, is not susceptible to being directly invoked before the courts of the EU or EU Member States. The European Commission ("the Commission") has justified this provision by underlining that it is important for the WTO Agreement and its annexes not to have a direct effect, that is one whereby natural or legal persons could invoke it under national law. The Commission further stated that private individuals and companies do not have similar rights in the United States and many other trading partners of the EU. The Commission concluded that without an express stipulation of such exclusion in the EU, a major imbalance would arise in the actual management of the obligations of the EU and other countries, as the EU would appear to be taking a very "pro-WTO" position in judicial terms. (N.B. in contrast, Article XX of the public procurement code specifically provides for challenge procedures at the national level for private individuals).

However, it would be an over-simplification to conclude that, on the basis of the case law mentioned above, private entities may not rely on GATT/WTO rules at all. Indeed, the ECJ has held in many instances in the past that GATT/WTO rules form an integral part of EU law. The European Institutions and the EU Member States are bound by these rules. A review of the legality of European institutions' activities can and must involve a determination as to whether such acts comply with GATT/WTO rules. The ECJ has, therefore, confirmed that individuals may rely on GATT/WTO provisions when challenging the validity of acts of European Institutions before the ECJ and the European Court of First Instance. Indeed, the ECJ expressly held that GATT (and consequently the WTO) would remain enforceable in cases where the EU intended to implement a particular obligation entered into within the framework of GATT, or if an EU act expressly refers to specific provisions of GATT. Thus, for example, private entities may challenge the validity of specific EU regulations imposing anti-dumping duties before the ECJ, by having reference to the inconsistency of such regulations with the WTO Anti-Dumping Code. It is important to note, however, that such actions for annulment of acts of European institutions may only be submitted to the ECJ and not courts of EU Member States.

Political sensitivities will, undoubtedly, influence further progress, in the EU and in other significant trading partners of the EU, towards "legalising" the WTO. Indeed, the EU, the United States, Japan, etc. may reach an agreement, in the future, allowing private entities in their respective jurisdictions to directly invoke GATT/WTO rules before national courts in an equivalent manner. It would appear, however, that no such move is envisaged for the near future.

C.8   *Future Developments*

C.8.1   Agriculture

Further liberalisation of the agricultural sector is predicted in the short to medium term.

C.8.2   Competition Policy

It appears that it will be difficult to establish substantive rules on competition policy at a WTO level, given the wide discrepancy of WTO members' views on this matter, as well as underlying fundamental differences at a political level. A likely development, therefore, will be the establishment of a framework for consultation and cooperation procedures between competition authorities of Members aiming at a coherent and consistent approach when dealing with business practices infringing national competition rules and having a negative impact on the proper functioning of the WTO, international trade and the benefits accruing to Members thereby. Such a framework may use an agreement currently in place between the EU and the US as a model.

The Singapore Ministerial Conference agreed to establish a working group to study issues raised by Members relating to the interaction between trade and competition policy, including anti-competitive practices, in order to identify any areas that may merit further consideration in the WTO framework.

C.8.3   Environment

The impact of environmental matters on world trade is expected to grow considerably during the course of the next decade. Increased awareness of the environmental damage caused by industry has already led to an explosion of legislation in developed countries. There was no specific environmental agreement arising out of the Uruguay Round, (although both the Agreements on Sanitary and Phytosanitary Measures and Technical Barriers to Trade contain significant environmental clauses) but, the importance of environmental matters was confirmed by a Ministerial Decision on Trade and the Environment issued at Marrakesh, prioritising the discussion of links between trade policies, environmental policies and sustainable development, at the WTO.

C.8.4   Trade-Related Investment Measures

A gradual but continual liberalisation of TRIMS can be expected. The agreement provides for consideration, by 1 January 2000, of whether it should be complemented by provisions on investment policy and competition policy.

C.8.5   On-Going Work Programme: Telecommunications, Maritime Transport, Movement of Natural Persons, Financial Services

At the end of the Uruguay Round Members agreed to continue negotiations in four basic areas whilst still enabling the Agreement on Trade in Services to be included in the Round. The four areas are basic telecommunications, maritime transport, movement of natural persons and financial services.

- Basic Telecommunications Services

Governments did not offer commitments during the Uruguay Round due mainly to the complex issues of privatisation of government monopolies arising in many countries. Sophisticated value-added telecommunications services, which are more commonly provided on a private basis, are however included in many GATS schedules.

68 WTO Members, accounting for more than 90% of world telecoms revenues, agreed on 15 February 1997 to open their markets to competition. The liberalisation of the markets will vary accordingly to each country's commitment with, for example, the EU, United States and Japan agreeing to open up their markets to domestic and foreign competition from 1 January 1998. Of the 68 countries which signed up to the agreement, 65 have adopted common rules to ensure fair competition in their telecoms markets. These rules will be enforceable through the Dispute Settlement Body.

- Maritime Transport

Negotiations were scheduled to end on 30 June 1996. The aim was to improve on commitments already included in the schedules covering the three main areas in this sector: access to and use of port facilities; auxiliary services; and ocean transport.

The multilateral efforts to conclude an agreement has suffered a serious setback. On 18 June 1996 the US delegation formally rejected a series of market opening measures as presented by the EU and 24 other countries. Given the United States' persistent refusal to participate in an agreement, the 50 or so countries involved in the talks are now trying to find a way to resume negotiations at a later date. They are most likely to re-incorporate maritime transport into the general cycle for further liberalisation of world trade, expected to begin in about 2000.

- Movement of Natural Persons

This relates to the entry and temporary stay of persons for the purpose of providing a service. It was agreed that negotiations to improve commitments would take place in the six months after the WTO came into force. On 25 June 1996 the EU Council adopted the Third Protocol which deals with this agreement, thus concluding the internal procedures for approving the agreement.

- Financial Services

Negotiations on financial services concessions were due to have been completed by 30 June 1995. However, the United States remained deeply unhappy at the refusal of other Members (particularly amongst the developing countries) to improve their concessions. The result was that the United States threatened to, and did, pull out of the financial trade negotiations when no "satisfactory" improvements were made by the 30 June deadline. (N.B. its current policy is to offer access to its financial services markets only to those countries that have made reciprocal concessions). The EU has attempted to save the financial services negotiations by stating that it is better to have an agreement on financial services, albeit an imperfect one, than to have no agreement at all. It has stressed that to give up at this stage would put back liberalisation and regulation of the financial market by a number of years. The EU's compromise deal is that Members should maintain their previously made pledges for an agreed number of years in order to secure an interim agreement that can then subsequently be built upon. At present, it appears likely that with or without US involvement, some form of compromise deal for the financial services sector will be agreed and that this, important, element of the Uruguay Round will be preserved. On 25 June 1996 the EU concluded its internal procedures for adopting the agreement.

At the Singapore Ministerial Conference WTO Members committed themselves to resuming negotiations in April 1997 with the aim of achieving significantly improved market access commitments with a broader level of participation in the agreed time frame.

CONCLUSION

The achievements of the Uruguay Round have laid the foundation for the creation of a truly global market for goods and services; one with a minimum of trade restrictions and a maximum of competition. However, whether this foundation can be fully built upon depends to a great extent on the ability of the WTO to administer successfully, promote and police the updated system for world trade. Of these three important elements of the WTO's role, it is its ability to police the Multilateral Trade Agreements that must be most open to question, and yet, whose proper functioning is arguably the most vital.

The failure of GATT's Dispute Settlement Mechanism to prevent its contracting parties from breaching GATT rules, and from taking unilateral action in trade disputes, was at the heart of its ultimate downfall as an organisation for regulating and promoting the liberalisation of world trade.

The dispute settlement mechanism is a much strengthened version of its GATT predecessor but is still entirely reliant upon the goodwill of Members to, firstly, refer disputes to it and secondly, to respect its recommendations.

This respect is absolutely essential. Should the major trading nations, such as the United States, Japan and the EU decide to follow their obligations to use the Dispute Settlement Mechanism and then abide by the recommendations of the DSB, the WTO will gain in stature and credibility, and the chances of building on the Uruguay Round foundations will be considerably enhanced. However, if Members, and particularly the major trading nations, choose to ignore the new dispute settlement mechanism, the world trading system could well fragment and fall apart. Destabilisation of the world trade system is not in the interest of any commercial organisation and companies have a major role to play in persuading their governments that respect for the WTO disputes system is essential for a successful WTO, and that a successful WTO is essential for the continued expansion and liberalisation of world trade.

BIBLIOGRAPHY

AND OTHER USEFUL PUBLICATIONS

WTO Publications
Focus — Monthly Newsletter.
Guide to GATT Law and Practice, (1995).
Trading into the Future, (1995).
Final Act Embodying the Results of the Uruguay Round of Multilateral
Trade Negotiations — Signed at Marrakech 15 April 1994.

European Commission Publications
What is the Community's Trade Barrier Regulation? (1996).
The Uruguay Round — Global Agreement, Global Benefits (1994).

Journals
Common Market Law Review,
(Kluwer Law International: published six times per year).
European Foreign Affairs Review,
(Kluwer Law International: published four times per year).
Journal of World Trade,
(Kluwer Law International: published six times per year).

Other Publications
McGovern, E., International Trade Regulation,
(Globefield Press: Loose-leaf, regularly updated).
Pescatore, P. et al, Handbook of GATT (WTO) Dispute Settlement,
(Kluwer Law International: Loose-leaf, regularly updated).
Stewart, T., (Editor), The World Trade Organization: The Multi-lateral
Trade Framework for the 21st Century,
(The American Bar Association: 1996).
van Houtte, H., The Law of International Trade, (Sweet & Maxwell: 1995).

ANNEX 1

OVERVIEW OF THE STATE-OF-PLAY OF WTO DISPUTES

(as of 11 February 1997)

	Consultation Requests	Distinct Matters	Active Cases	Completed Cases	Settled or Inactive Cases
TOTAL	66	45	9	2	15

1. APPELLATE REPORTS ADOPTED

(1)   *United States - Standards for Reformulated and Conventional Gasoline*, complaints by Venezuela (WT/DS2) and Brazil (WT/DS4). A single panel considered the complaints of both Venezuela and Brazil. Complainants alleged that a US gasoline regulation discriminated against complainants' gasoline in violation of GATT Articles I and III and Article 2 of the Agreement on Technical Barriers to Trade (TBT). The report of the panel found the regulation to be inconsistent with GATT Article III:4 and not to benefit from an Article XX exception, (WT/DS2/R, 29 January 1996). The United States appealed on 21 February 1996. ON 22 April, the Appellate Body issued its report (WT/DS2/AB/R), modifying the panel report on the interpretation of GATT Article XX(g), but concluding that the Article XX(g) was not applicable in this case. The Appellate Report, together with the panel report as modified by the Appellate Report, was adopted by the DSB on 20 May 1996.

(2)   *Japan - Taxes on Alcoholic Beverages*, complaints by the European Communities (WT/DS8), Canada (WT/DS10) and the United States (WT/DS11). Complainants claimed that spirits exported to Japan were discriminated against under the Japanese liquor tax system which, in their view, levies a substantially lower tax on "shochu" than on whisky, cognac and white spirits. A joint panel was established at the DSB meeting on 27 September 1995. The report of the panel, which found the Japanese tax system to be inconsistent

with GATT Article III:2, was circulated to Members on 11 July 1996. On 8 August 1996 Japan filed an appeal. The report of the Appellate Body was circulated to Members on 4 October 1996. The Appellate Body's Report affirmed the Panel's conclusion that the Japanese Liquor Tax Law is inconsistent with GATT Article III:2, but pointed out several areas where the Panel had erred in its legal reasoning. The Appellate Report, together with the panel report as modified by the Appellate Report, was adopted on 1 November 1996.

2. APPELLATE REPORT ISSUED

(1)   *United States - Restrictions on Imports of Cotton and Man-Made Fibre Underwear,* complaint by Costa Rica (WT/DS24). This dispute involves US restrictions on textile imports from Costa Rica, allegedly in violation of the ATC agreement. The Panel found that the US restraints were not valid. The report of the panel was circulated to members on 8 November 1996. On 11 November 1996, Costa Rica notified its decision to appeal against one aspect of the Panel report. The Appellate Body upheld the appeal by Costa Rica on that particular point. The report of the Appellate Body was circulated to Members on 10 February 1997.

3. PANEL REPORT APPEALED

(1)   *Brazil - Measures Affecting Desiccated Coconut,* complaint by the Philippines (WT/DS22). The Philippines claims that the countervailing duty imposed by Brazil on the Philippine's exports of desiccated coconut is inconsistent with WTO and GATT rules. The report of the Panel concluded that the provisions of the agreements relied on by the claimant were inapplicable to the dispute (WT/DS22/R). The report was circulated to members on 17 October 1996. On 16 December 1996, the Philippines notified its decision to appeal against certain issues of law and legal interpretations developed by the panel.

4. PANEL REPORT ISSUED

(1)   *United States - Measure Affecting Imports of Woven Wool Shirts and Blouses,* complaint by India (WT/DS33). This case concerns the transitional safeguard measure imposed by the United States. India claimed that the safeguard measure is inconsistent with Articles 2, 6

and 8 of the ATC. A panel was established at the DSB meeting on 17 April 1996. The panel found that the safeguard measure imposed by the United States violated the provisions of the ATC. The report of the panel was circulated to Members on 6 January 1997.

5.   ACTIVE PANELS

(1)   *European Communities - Regime for the Importation, Sale and Distribution of Bananas*, complaints by Ecuador, Guatemala, Honduras, Mexico and the United States (WT/DS27). The complainants in this case other than Ecuador had requested consultations with the EC on the same issue on 28 September 1995 (WT/DS16). After Ecuador's accession to the WTO, the current complainants again requested consultations with the EC on 5 February 1996. The complainants allege that the EC's regime for importation, sale and distribution of bananas is inconsistent with GATT Articles I, II, III, X, XI and XIII as well as provisions of the Import Licensing Agreement, the Agreement on Agriculture, the TRIMs Agreement and the GATS. A panel was established at the DSB meeting on 8 May 1996.

(2)(a)   *European Communities - Measures Affecting Meat and Meat Products* (Hormones), complaint by the United States (WT/DS26). In a communication dated 25 April 1996, the United States requested the establishment of a panel, claiming that measures taken by the EC under the Council Directive Prohibiting the Use of Livestock Farming of Certain Substances Having a Hormonal Action restrict or prohibit imports of meat and meat products from the United States, and are apparently inconsistent with GATT Articles III or XI, SPS Agreement Articles 2, 3 and 5, TBT Agreement Article 2 and the Agreement on Agriculture Article 4. A panel was established at the DSB meeting on 20 May 1996.

(2)(b)   *European Communities - Measures Affecting Livestock and Meat* (Hormones), complaint by Canada (WT/DS48). On 28 June 1996, Canada requested consultations with the European Communities regarding the importation of livestock and meat from livestock that have been treated with certain substances having a hormonal action under GATT Article XXII and the corresponding provisions in the SPS, TBT and Agriculture Agreements. Violations of SPS Articles 2, 3 and 5; GATT Article III or XI; TBT Article 2; and Agriculture Article 4 are alleged. The Canadian claim is essentially the same as the US claim (WT/DS26), for which a panel was established earlier. See above. The DSB established a panel on 16 October 1996.

(3)   Canada - Certain Measures Concerning Periodicals, complaint by the United States (WT/DS31). In its request for consultations dated 11 March 1996, the United States claims that measures prohibiting or restricting the importation into Canada of certain periodicals are in contravention of GATT Article XI. The US further alleges that the tax treatment of so-called "split-run" periodicals and the application of favourable postage rates to certain Canadian periodicals are inconsistent with GATT Article III. The DSB established a panel on 19 June 1996.

(4)   *Japan - Measures Affecting Consumer Photographic Film and Paper*, complaint by the United States (WT/DS44). On 13 June 1996, the United States requested consultations with Japan concerning Japan's laws, regulations and requirements affecting the distribution, offering for sale and internal sale of imported consumer photographic film and paper. The US alleges that the Japanese Government treated imported film and paper less favourably through these measures, in violation of GATT Articles III and X. The US also alleges that these measures nullify or impair benefits accruing to the US (a non-violation claim). See also 7(6) below. The United States requested the establishment of a panel on 20 September 1996 and it was established on 16 October 1996.

(5)   *United States - The Cuban Liberty and Democratic Solidarity Act*, complaint by the European Communities (WT/DS38). On 3 May 1996 the European Communities requested consultations with the United States concerning the Cuban Liberty and Democratic Solidarity (LIBERTAD) Act of 1996 and other legislation enacted by the US Congress regarding trade sanctions against Cuba. The EC claims that US trade restrictions on goods of Cuban origin, as well as the possible refusal of visas and the exclusion of non-US nationals from US territory, are inconsistent with the US obligations under the WTO Agreement. Violations of GATT Articles I, III, V, XI and XIII, and GATS Articles I, III, VI, XVI and XVII are alleged. The EC also alleges that even if these measures by the US may not be in violation of specific provisions of GATT or GATS, they nevertheless nullify or impair its expected benefits under GATT 1994 and GATS and impede the attainment of the objectives of GATT 1994. The European Communities requested the establishment of a panel on 3 October 1996. The DSB established a panel at its meeting on 20 November 1996.

(6)   *India - Patent Protection for Pharmaceutical and Agricultural Chemical Products*, complaint by the United States (WT/DS50). This request, dated 2 July 1996, concerns the alleged absence of patent pro-

tection for pharmaceutical and agricultural chemical products in India. Violations of the TRIPS Agreement Articles 27, 65 and 70 are claimed. The United States requested the establishment of a panel on 7 November 1996. The DSB established a panel at its meeting on 20 November 1996.

6. ESTABLISHMENT OF PANELS REQUESTED

(1)   *Pakistan - Patent Protection for Pharmaceutical and Agricultural Chemical Products,* complaint by the United States (WT/DS36). In its request for consultations dated 30 April 1996, the United States claimed that the absence in Pakistan of (i) either patent protection for pharmaceutical and agricultural chemical products or a system to permit the filing of applications for patents on these products and (ii) a system to grant exclusive marketing rights in such products, violates TRIPS Agreement Articles 27, 65 and 70. On 4 July 1996, the United States requested the establishment of a panel. The DSB considered the request at its meeting on 16 July 1996, but did not establish a panel due to Pakistan's objection.

(2)   *Brazil - Export Financing Programme for Aircraft,* complaint by Canada (WT/DS46). On 19 June 1996, Canada requested consultations with Brazil, based on Article 4 of the Subsidies Agreement, which provides for special procedures for export subsidies. Canada claims that export subsidies granted under the Brazilian Programa de Financiamento às Exportaçóes (PROEX), to foreign purchasers of Brazil's Embraer aircraft are inconsistent with the Subsidies Agreement Articles 3, 27.4 and 27.5. Canada requested the establishment of a panel on 16 September 1996, alleging violations of both the Subsidies Agreement and GATT 1994. The DSB considered this request at its meeting on 27 September 1996. Due to Brazil's objection to the establishment of a panel, Canada agreed to modify its request, limiting the scope to the Subsidies Agreement. the modified request was issued by Canada on 3 October 1996.

(3)   *European Communities - Duties on Imports of Grains,* complaint by the United States (WT/DS13). This request for consultations, dated 19 July 1995, has potentially broader product coverage than the case brought by Canada (WT/DS9, item 8(5)(a) below) but otherwise concerns much the same issues. On 28 September 1995, the United States requested the establishment of a panel to be considered at the meeting of the DSB on 11 October 1995, but the EC objected to

it. The United States again requested the establishment of a panel to be considered at the meeting of the DSB on 3 December 1996, but later dropped the request at the meeting.

(4)   *Hungary - Export Subsidies in Respect of Agricultural Products*, complaint by Argentina, Australia, Canada, New Zealand, Thailand and the United States (WT/DS35). This request, dated 27 March 1996, claims that Hungary violated the Agreement on Agriculture (Article 3.3 and Part V) by providing export subsidies in respect of agricultural products not specified in its Schedule, as well as by providing agricultural export subsidies in excess of its commitment levels. On 9 January 1997, Argentina, Australia, New Zealand and the United States requested the establishment of a panel.

(5)   *Argentina - Certain Measures Affecting Imports of Footwear, Textiles, Apparel and Other Items*, complaint by the United States (WT/DS56). This request, dated 4 October 1996, concerns the imposition of specific duties on these items in excess of the bound rate and other measures by Argentina. The United States contends that these measures violate Articles II, VII, VIII and X of GATT 1994, Article 2 of the TBT Agreement, Article 1 to 8 of the Agreement on the Implementation of Article VII of GATT 1994, and Article 7 of the Agreement on Textiles and Clothing. On 9 January 1997, the United States requested the establishment of a panel.

(6)   *Turkey - Taxation of Foreign Film Revenues*, complaint by the United States (WT/DS43). This request for consultations, dates 12 June 1996, concerns Turkey's taxation of revenues generated from the showing of foreign films. Violation of GATT Article III is alleged. On 9 January 1997, the United States requested the establishment of a panel.

(7)   *United States - Import Prohibition of Certain Shrimp and Shrimp Products*, complaint by India, Malaysia, Pakistan and Thailand (WT/DS58). This request, dated 8 October 1996, concerns a joint complaint by India, Malaysia, Pakistan and Thailand against a ban on importation of shrimp and shrimp products from these countries imposed by the United States under Section 609 of US Public Law 101-62. Violations of Articles I, XI and XIII of GATT 1994, as well as nullification and impairment of benefits, are alleged. On 9 January 1997, Malaysia and Thailand requested the establishment of a panel. On 30 January 1997, Pakistan also requested the establishment of a panel.

(8)   *Guatemala - Anti-Dumping Investigation Regarding Imports of Portland Cement from Mexico,* complaint by Mexico (WT/DS60). This request, dated 15 October 1996 is in respect of an anti-dumping investigation commenced by Guatemala with regard to imports of portland cement from Mexico. Mexico alleges that this investigation is in violation of Guatemala's obligations under Articles 2, 3, 5 and 7.1 of the Anti-Dumping Agreement. On 4 February 1997, Mexico requested the establishment of a panel.

7.   PENDING CONSULTATIONS

(1)(a)   Korea - Measures Concerning the Testing and Inspection of Agricultural Products, complaint by the United States (WT/DS3). Request circulated on 6 April 1995. The dispute involves testing and inspection requirements with respect to imports of agricultural products into Korea. The measures are alleged to be in violation of GATT Articles III or XI, Articles 2 and 5 of the Agreement on Sanitary and Phytosanitary Measures (SPS), TBT Articles 5 and 6 and Agriculture Article 4. See below.

(1)(b)   *Korea - Measures Concerning Inspection of Agricultural Products,* complaint by the United States (WT/DS41). This request for consultations, dated 24 May 1996, concerns testing, inspection and other measures required for the importation of agricultural products into Korea. The United States claims these measures restrict imports and appear to be inconsistent with the WTO Agreement. Violations of GATT Articles III and XI, SPS Articles 2, 5 and 8, TBT Articles 2, 5 and 6, and Article 4 of the Agreement on Agriculture are alleged. The United States requested consultations with Korea on similar issues on 4 April 1995 (WT/DS3/1). See above.

(2)(a)   *Australia - Measures Affecting the Importation of Salmon,* complaint by Canada (WT/DS18). This request for consultations, dated 5 October 1995, is about Australia's prohibition of imports on salmon from Canada based on a quarantine regulation. Canada alleges that the prohibition is inconsistent with GATT Articles XI and XIII and the SPS Agreement.

(2)(b)   *Australia - Measures Affecting the Importation of Salmonids,* complaint by the United States (WT/DS21). This request for consultations, dated 17 November 1995, concerns the same regulation alleged to be in violation of the WTO Agreements in WT/DS18. See above.

(3)(a)   *Turkey - Restrictions on Imports of Textile and Clothing Products*, complaint by Hong Kong (WT/DS29). This request, dated 12 February 1996, claims that Turkey's quantitative restrictions on imports of textile and clothing products are in violation of GATT Articles XI and XIII. The background to this dispute is a recently concluded customs union agreement between Turkey and the European Communities. Hong Kong claims that GATT Article XXIV does not entitle Turkey to impose new quantitative restrictions in the present case. See below.

(3)(b)   *Turkey - Restrictions on Imports of Textile and Clothing Products*, complaint by India (WT/DS34). This request, dated 21 March 1996, claims that Turkey's imposition of quantitative restrictions on imports of a broad range of textile and clothing products is inconsistent with GATT Articles XI and XIII, as well as ATC Article 2. Earlier, India had requested to be joined in the consultations between Hong Kong and Turkey on the same subject matter (WT/DS29). See above and below.

(3)(c)   *Turkey - Restrictions on Imports of Textile and Clothing Products*, complaint by Thailand (WT/DS47). This request for consultations, dated 20 June 1996, concerns Turkey's imposition of quantitative restrictions on imports of textile and clothing products from Thailand. Violations of GATT Articles I, II, XI and XIII as well as Article 2 of the Textiles Agreement are alleged. Earlier, Hong Kong (WT/DS29) and India (WT/DS34) separately requested consultations with Turkey on the same measure.

(4)   *Brazil - Countervailing Duties on Imports of Desiccated Coconut and Coconut Milk Powder from Sri Lanka*, complaint by Sri Lanka (WT/DS30). This request, dated 23 February 1996, claims that Brazil's imposition of countervailing duties on Sri Lanka's export of desiccated coconut and coconut milk powder is inconsistent with GATT Articles I, II and VI and Article 13(a) of the Agriculture Agreement (the so-called peace clause). See 3(1) above (WT/DS22).

(5)   *Korea - Laws, Regulations and Practices in the Telecommunications Sector*, complaint by the European Communities (WT/DS40). This request for consultations, dated 9 May 1996, concerns the laws, regulations and practices in the telecommunications sector. The EC claims that the procurement practices of the Korean telecommunications sector (Korea Telecom and Dacom) discriminate against foreign suppliers. The EC also claims that the Korean govern-

ment has favoured US suppliers under two bilateral telecommunications agreements between Korea and the US. Violations of GATT Articles I, III and XVII are alleged.

(6)   *Japan - Measures Affecting Distribution Services*, complaint by the United States (WT/DS45). This request, dated 13 June 1996, concerns Japan's measures affecting distribution services (not limited to the photographic film and paper sector) through the operation of the Large-Scale Retail Store Law, which regulates the floor space, business hours and holidays of supermarkets and department stores. Violations of the GATS Article III (Transparency) and Article XVI (Market Access) are alleged. The US also alleges that these measures nullify or impair benefits accruing to the US (a non-violation claim). See 5(4) above. The United States requested further consultations with Japan on 20 September 1996, expanding the factual and legal basis of its claim.

(7)(a)   *Brazil - Certain Automotive Investment Measures*, complaint by Japan (WT/DS51). This request, dated 30 July 1996, concerns certain automotive investment measures taken by the Brazilian government. Violations of the TRIMs Agreement Article 2, GATT Articles I:1 and III:4 as well as the Subsidies Agreement Articles 3 and 27.4 are alleged. In addition, the United States also makes a non-violation claim under GATT Article XXIII:1(b).

(7)(b)   *Brazil - Certain Measures Affecting Trade and Investment in the Automotive Sector*, complaint by the United States (WT/DS52). this request, dated 9 August 1996, concerns the same measures as identified in Japan's request above. Violations of the TRIMs Agreement Article 2, GATT Articles I:1 and III:4 as well as the Subsidies Agreement Articles 3 and 27.4 are alleged. In addition, the United States also makes a non-violation claim under GATT Article XXIII:1(b).

(7)(c)   *Brazil - Certain Measures Affecting Trade and Investment in the Automotive Sector*, complaint by the United States (WT/DS65). This request, dated 10 January 1997, concerns more or less the same measures as in WT/DS52 above. However, this request also includes measures adopted by Brazil subsequent to consultations held with the United States pursuant to the request under WT/DS52, which measures confer benefits to certain companies located in Japan, the Republic of Korea, and the European Communities. The United States alleges violations under Articles I:1 and III:4 of GATT 1994, Article 2 of the TRIMs Agreement, and Articles 3 and 27.4 of the SCM Agreement. The United

States has also made a nullification and impairment of benefits claim under Article XXIII:1(b) of GATT 1994.

(8)   *Mexico - Customs Valuation of Imports*, complaint by the European Communities (WT/DS53). This request, dated 27 August 1996, concerns the Mexican Customs Law. The EC claims that Mexico applies CIF value as the basis of customs valuation of imports originating in non-NAFTA countries, while it applies FOB value for imports originating in NAFTA countries. Violation of GATT Article XXIV:5(b) is alleged.

(9)(a)   *Indonesia - Certain Measures Affecting the Automobile Industry*, complaint by the European Communities (WT/DS54). This request, dated 3 October 1996, concerns the exemption from customs duties and luxury taxes by Indonesia, on imports of "national vehicles" and components thereof, and related measures. The EC contends that these measures are in violation of Indonesia's obligations under Articles I and III of GATT 1994, Article 2 of the TRIMs Agreement and Articles 3 of the SCM Agreement.

(9)(b)   *Indonesia - Certain Measures Affecting the Automobile Industry*, complaint by Japan (WT/DS55). This request, dated 4 October 1996, concerns Indonesia's National Car Programme - basically the same measures as in WT/DS54. Japan contends that these measures are in violation of Indonesia's obligations under Articles I:1, III:2 and X:3(a) of GATT 1994, as well as Articles 2 and 5.4 of the TRIMs Agreement.

(9)(c)   *Indonesia - Certain Measures Affecting the Automobile Industry*, complaint by the United States (WT/DS59). This request, dated 8 October 1996, concerns Indonesia's National Car Programme - basically the same measures being complained of in WT/DS54. The United States contends that these measures are in violation of Indonesia's obligations under Articles I and III of GATT 1994, Article 2 of the TRIMs Agreement, Articles 3, 6 and 28 of the SCM Agreement and Articles 3, 20 and 65 of the TRIPS Agreement. See above.

(9)(d)   *Indonesia - Certain Measures Affecting the Automobile Industry*, complaint by Japan (WT/DS64). This request, dated 29 November 1996, is in respect of Indonesia's National Car Programme - the same measures the subject of complaints in WT/DS54, 55 and 59. In its earlier request for consultations on these measures (WT/DS55) Japan had confined itself to violations under GATT and TRIMs. In this request Japan is now alleging violations of Articles 3, 6 and 28 of the SCM Agreement.

(10)   *United States - Import Prohibition of Certain Shrimp and Shrimp Products*, complaint by the Philippines (WT/DS61). This request, dated 25 October 1996, is in respect of a complaint by the Philippines regarding a ban on the importation of certain shrimp and shrimp products from the Philippines imposed by the United States under Section 609 of U.S. Public Law 101-62. Violations of Articles I, II, III, VIII, XI and XIII of GATT 1994 and Article 2 of the TBT Agreement are alleged. A nullification and impairment of benefits under GATT 1994 is also alleged. See also 5(7) (WT/DS58).

(11)   *European Communities - Customs Classification of Certain Computer Equipment*, complaint by the United States (WT/DS62). This request, dated 8 November 1996, is in respect of the reclassification by the European Communities, for tariff purposes, of certain Local Area Network (LAN) adapter equipment and personal computers with multimedia capability. The United States alleges that these measures violate Article II of GATT 1994.

(12)   *United States - Anti-Dumping Measures on Imports of Solid Urea from the Former German Democratic Republic*, complaint by the European Communities (WT/DS63). This request, dated 28 November 1996, is in respect of Anti-Dumping duties imposed on exports of solid urea from the former German Democratic Republic by the United States. The EC contends that these measures violate Articles 9 and 11 of the Anti-Dumping Agreement.

(13)   *Japan - Measures Affecting Imports of Pork*, complaint by the European Communities, (WT/DS66). This request, dated 15 January 1997, is in respect of certain measures affecting imports of pork and its processed products imposed by Japan. The EC contends that these measures are in violation of Japan's obligations under Articles I, X:3 and XIII of the GATT 1994. The EC also contends that these measures nullify or impair benefits accruing to it under the GATT 1994.

8.   Settled Cases or Inactive Panels

(1)   *Malaysia - Prohibition of Imports of Polyethylene and Polypropylene*, complaint by Singapore (WT/DS1). This, the first dispute under the WTO's dispute settlement procedures, was settled on 19 July 1995, with Singapore's withdrawal of the panel request.

(2)   *Korea - Measures concerning the Shelf-life of Products*, complaint

by the United States (WT/DS5). The parties notified a mutually acceptable solution to this dispute on 31 July 1995.

(3)   *United States - Imposition of Import Duties on Automobiles from Japan under Sections 301 and 304 of the Trade Act of 1974*, complaint by Japan (WT/DS6). On 19 July 1995, the parties notified settlement of this dispute. Japan had alleged that the import surcharges violated GATT Articles I and II.

(4)   *Japan - Measures Affecting the Purchase of Telecommunications Equipment,* complaint by the European Communities (WT/DS15). This request for consultations, dated 18 August 1995, claims that a 1994 agreement reached between the United States and Japan concerning telecommunications equipment is inconsistent with GATT Articles I:1, III:4 and XVII:1(c), and nullifies or impairs benefits accruing to the EC. The United States has joined in the consultations. Although there has been no official notification, the case appears to have been settled bilaterally.

(5)(a)   *European Communities - Duties on Imports of Cereals*, complaint by Canada (WT/DS9). Canada requested consultations with the EC on 10 July 1995 concerning EC regulations implementing some of the EC's Uruguay Round concessions on agriculture, specifically, regulations which impose a duty on wheat imports based on reference prices rather than transaction values, with the result that the duty-paid import price for Canadian wheat will be greater than the effective intervention price increased by 55% whenever the transaction value is greater than the representative price. A panel was established at the DSB meeting on 11 October 1995, but no panelists have been selected.

(5)(b)   *European Communities - Duties on Imports of Rice*, complaint by Thailand (WT/DS17). This request for consultations, dated 3 October 1995, covers more or less the same grounds as Canadian (WT/DS9) and the US (WT/DS13) complaints over the EC duties on grains ((5)(a) and 5(3) above). In addition, Thailand seems to have alleged that the EC has violated the most-favoured-nation requirement under GATT Article I in their preferential treatment of basmati rice from India and Pakistan. See also the Uruguayan complaint (WT/DS25, (5)(c) below).

(5)(c)   *European Communities - Implementation of the Uruguay Round Commitments Concerning Rice*, complaint by Uruguay

(WT/DS25). This request for consultations, dated 18 December 1995, seems similar to the claim by Thailand (WT/DS17, (5)(b) above).

(6)   *Venezuela - Anti-Dumping Investigation in Respect of Imports of Certain Oil Country Tubular Goods (OCTG)*, complaint by Mexico (WT/DS23), dated 5 December 1995. This case appears to have been settled because of Venezuela's termination of the anti-dumping investigation.

(7)   *Korea - Measures Concerning Bottled Water*, complaint by Canada (WT/DS20). In this dispute, Canada claimed that Korean regulations on the shelf-life and physical treatment (disinfection) of bottled water were inconsistent with GATT Articles III and XI, SPS Articles 2 and 5 and TBT Article 2. At the DSB meeting on 24 April 1996, the parties to the dispute announced that they reached a settlement.

(8)   *United States - Measures Affecting Imports of Women's and Girls' Wool Coats*, complaint by India (WT/DS32). In a communication dated 14 March 1996, India requested the establishment of a panel, claiming that the transitional safeguard measures on these textile products by the United States were inconsistent with ATC Articles 2, 6 and 8. A panel was established in the DSB meeting on 17 April 1996. However, on 25 April 1996, India requested "termination of further action in pursuance of the decision taken by the DSB on 17 April 1996 to establish a panel" in light of the US removal of the safeguard measures on these products, which came into effect from 24 April 1996.

(9)   *European Communities - Trade Description of Scallops*, complaints by Canada (WT/DS7), Peru (WT/DS12) and Chile (WT/DS14). The complaint concerns a French Government Order laying down the official name and trade description of scallops. Complainants claim that this Order will reduce competitiveness on the French market as their product will no longer be able to be sold as "Coquille Saint-Jacques" although there is no difference between their scallops and French scallops in terms of colour, size, texture, appearance and use, i.e. it is claimed they are "like products". Violations of GATT Articles I and III and TBT Article 2 are alleged. A panel was established at the request of Canada on 19 July 1995. A joint panel was established on 11 October 1995 at the request of Peru and Chile on the same subject. The two panels have concluded their substantive work, but they suspended the proceedings pursuant to Article 12.12 of the DSU in May

1996 in view of the consultations held among the parties concerned toward a mutually agreed solution. The parties notified a mutually agreed solution to the DSB on 5 July 1996. Brief panel reports noting the settlement were circulated to Members on 5 August 1996 in accordance with the provisions of Article 12.7 of the DSU.

(10)   *United States - Tariff Increases on Products from the European Communities*, complaint by the European Communities (WT/DS39). In its request for consultations, dated 17 April 1996, the EC claimed that the measures taken under the Presidential Proclamation No. 5759 of 24 December 1987 (retaliation against the "hormones" directive), which resulted in tariff increases on products from the European Communities, are inconsistent with GATT Articles I, II and XXIII, as well as DSU Articles 3, 22 and 23. On 19 June 1996, the EC requested the establishment of a panel. In its request, the EC further claimed that the United States apparently failed to "ensure the conformity of its laws, regulations and administrative procedures with its obligations" under the WTO, with respect to the application of Section 301 of the 1974 Trade Act in this case (WTO Agreement Article XVI:4). The United States withdrew the measure on 15 July 1996, and the EC decided not to pursue its panel request, reserving its rights to reconvene, if necessary, a further meeting of the DSB at an early date.

(11)   *Poland - Import Regime for Automobiles*, complaint by India (WT/DS19). This request for consultations, dated 28 September 1995, concerns Poland's preferential treatment of the EC in its tariff scheme on automobiles. On 16 July 1996, both parties notified a mutually agreed solution to the DSB.

(12)   *Portugal - Patent Protection under the Industrial Property Act*, complaint by the United States (WT/DS37). This request for consultations dated 30 April 1996, concerned Portugal's term of patent protection under its Industrial Property Act. The US claimed that the provisions in that Act with respect to existing patents were inconsistent with Portugal's obligations under the TRIPS Agreement. Violations under Articles 33, 65 and 70 were alleged. On 3 October 1996, both parties notified a mutually agreed solution to the DSB.

(13)   *United States - Anti-Dumping Investigation Regarding Imports of Fresh or Chilled Tomatoes from Mexico*, complaint by Mexico (WT/DS49). On 1 July 1996, Mexico requested consultations with the United States regarding the anti-dumping investigation on fresh and chilled tomatoes imported from Mexico under Article 17.3 of the

Anti-dumping Agreement. Violations of GATT Articles VI and X as well as Articles 2, 3, 5, 6 and 7.1 of the Anti-dumping Agreement are alleged. Mexico claims this to be a case of urgency, where the expedited procedures under Articles 4.8 and 4.9 of the DSU are applicable. US Commerce Department official releases indicate that the case has been settled.

(14)   *Australia - Textiles, Clothing and Footwear Import Credit Scheme*, complaint by the United States (WT/DS57). This request, dated 7 October 1996, concerns a complaint by the United States against subsidies being granted and maintained by Australia on leather products under the TCF scheme. A violation of Article 3 of the SCM Agreement is alleged. The US is also invoking Article 30 of the SCM Agreement to the extent that it incorporates by reference Article XXIII:1 of GATT 1994. An official release from the USTR in Washington on 25 November 1996 indicates that the case has been settled.

(15)(a)   *Japan - Measures Concerning Sound Recordings*, complaint by the United States (WT/DS28). This request, dated 9 February 1996, is the first WTO dispute settlement case involving the TRIPS Agreement. The United States claims that Japan's copyright regime for the protection of intellectual property in sound recordings is inconsistent with, inter alia, the TRIPS Agreement Article 14 (protection of performers, producers of phonograms and broadcasting organisations). On January 24 1997, both parties informed the DSB that they had reached a mutually satisfactory solution to the dispute.

(15)(b)   *Japan - Measures Concerning Sound Recordings*, complaint by the European communities (WT/DS42). This request for consultations, dated 24 May 1996, concerns the intellectual property protection of sound recordings under GATT Article XXII:1. Violations of Articles 14.6 and 70.2 of the TRIPS Agreement are alleged. Earlier, the United States requested consultations with Japan on the same issue (WT/DS28), in which the EC joined. This dispute appears to have been settled.

ANNEX 2

MEMBERSHIP OF THE WORLD TRADE ORGANIZATION

(as of 29 January 1997)

GOVERNMENT	DATE OF ENTRY INTO FORCE/MEMBERSHIP
Angola	23 November 1996
Antigua and Barbuda	1 January 1995
Argentina	1 January 1995
Australia	1 January 1995
Austria	1 January 1995
Bahrain	1 January 1995
Bangladesh	1 January 1995
Barbados	1 January 1995
Belgium	1 January 1995
Belize	22 February 1996
Benin	22 February 1996
Bolivia	13 September 1995
Botswana	31 May 1995
Brazil	1 January 1995
Brunei Darussalam	1 January 1995
Bulgaria	1 December 1996
Burkina Faso	3 June 1995
Burundi	23 July 1995
Cameroon	13 December 1995
Canada	1 January 1995
Central African Republic	31 May 1995
Chad	19 October 1996
Chile	1 January 1995
Colombia	30 April 1995
Costa Rica	1 January 1995
Cote d'Ivoire	1 January 1995
Cuba	20 April 1995
Cyprus	30 July 1995

Czech Republic	1	January	1995
Denmark	1	January	1995
Djibouti	31	May	1995
Dominica	1	January	1995
Dominican Republic	9	March	1995
Ecuador	21	January	1996
Egypt	30	June	1995
El Salvador	7	May	1995
European Community	1	January	1995
Fiji	1	January	1995
Finland	1	January	1995
France	1	January	1995
Gabon	1	January	1995
Gambia	23	October	1996
Germany	1	January	1995
Ghana	1	January	1995
Greece	1	January	1995
Grenada	22	February	1996
Guatemala	21	July	1995
Guinea Bissau	31	May	1995
Guinea, Republic of	25	October	1995
Guyana	1	January	1995
Haiti	30	January	1995
Honduras	1	January	1995
Hong Kong	1	January	1995
Hungary	1	January	1995
Iceland	1	January	1995
India	1	January	1995
Indonesia	1	January	1995
Ireland	1	January	1995
Israel	21	April	1995
Italy	1	January	1995
Jamaica	9	March	1995
Japan	1	January	1995
Kenya	1	January	1995
Korea	1	January	1995
Kuwait	1	January	1995
Lesotho	31	May	1995
Lichtenstein	1	September	1995
Luxembourg	1	January	1995
Macau	1	January	1995
Madagascar	17	November	1995
Malawi	31	May	1995

Malaysia	1	January	1995
Maldives	31	May	1995
Mali	31	May	1995
Malta	1	January	1995
Mauritania	31	May	1995
Mauritius	1	January	1995
Mexico	1	January	1995
Mongolia	29	January	1997
Morocco	1	January	1995
Mozambique	26	August	1995
Myanmar	1	January	1995
Namibia	1	January	1995
Netherlands (Kingdom in Europe and the Netherlands Antilles)	1	January	1995
New Zealand	1	January	1995
Nicaragua	3	September	1995
Niger	1	January	1995
Nigeria	1	January	1995
Norway		1 January	1995
Pakistan	1	January	1995
Papua New Guinea	9	June	1996
Paraguay	1	January	1995
Peru	1	January	1995
Philippines	1	January	1995
Poland	1	July	1995
Portugal	1	January	1995
Qatar	13	January	1996
Romania	1	January	1995
Rwanda	22	May	1996
Saint Lucia	1	January	1995
Saint Kitts & Nevis	21	February	1996
Saint Vincent & the Grenadines	1	January	1995
Senegal	1	January	1995
Sierra Leone	23	July	1995
Singapore	1	January	1995
Slovak Republic	1	January	1995
Slovenia	30	July	1995
Solomon Islands	26	July	1996
South Africa	1	January	1995
Spain	1	January	1995
Sri Lanka	1	January	1995
Surinam	1	January	1995
Swaziland	1	January	1995
Sweden	1	January	1995

Switzerland	1	July	1995
Tanzania	1	January	1995
Thailand	1	January	1995
Togo	31	May	1995
Trinidad & Tobago	1	March	1995
Tunisia	29	March	1995
Turkey	26	March	1995
Uganda	1	January	1995
United Arab Emirates	10	April	1996
United Kingdom	1	January	1995
United States	1	January	1995
Uruguay	1	January	1995
Venezuela	1	January	1995
Zaire	1	January	1997
Zambia	1	January	1995
Zimbabwe	3	March	1995

Source: WTO

WORLD TRADE ORGANIZATION ACCESSIONS
(as of 29 January 1997)

The following 28 governments have requested to join the WTO. Their applications are currently being considered by accession working parties.

Albania	Macedonia (former Yugoslav republic of)
Algeria	Moldova
Armenia	Nepal
Belarus	Oman, Sultenate of
Cambodia	Russian Federation
People's Republic of China	Saudi Arabia
Croatia	Seychelles
Estonia	Sudan
Georgia	Chinese Taipei
Jordan	Tonga
Kazakstan	Ukraine
Kirgyg Republic	Uzbekistan
Latvia	Vanuatu
Lithuania	Vietnam

NB: Panama's Protocol of accession was approved by the General Council on 2 October 1996. Panama will become a WTO Member 30 days after the WTO receives confirmation of Panama's ratification

Source: WTO

105

ANNEX 3

CHAIRPERSONS OF COUNCILS, COMMITTEES AND WORKING PARTIES

(as at 7 February 1997)

At the WTO General Council meeting on 7 February 1997, the following were elected Chairpersons of their respective WTO bodies:

General Council	H.E. Mr. Celso Lafer (Brazil)
Dispute Settlement Body	H.E. Mr. Wade Armstong (New Zealand)
Trade Policy Review Body	H.E. Mr. Munir Akram (Pakistan)
Council for Trade in Goods	H.E. Mr. Terje Johannessen (Norway)
Council for Trade-Related Aspects of Intellectual Property Rights (TRIPs)	H.E. Mrs. Carmen Luz Guarda (Chile)
Council for Trade in Services	H.E. Mr. Joun Yung Sun (Korea)
Committee on Trade and the Environment	H.E. Mr. Björn Ekblom (Finland)
Committee on Trade and Developmen	H.E. Mr. Dhurmahdass Baichoo (Mauritius)
Committee on Budget, Finance and Administration	H.E. Mr. Kamel Morjane (Tunisia)

Committee on
Balance-of-Payments

Mr. Peter R Jenkins
(United Kingdom)

Committee on Regional
Trading Agreements

H.E. Mr. John Weekes
(Canada)

NB: At the time of going to press the remaining chairpersons of the WTO's working parties had yet to be chosen

ANNEX 4

LIST OF WTO MEMBER'S AMBASSADORS AND EMBASSIES

The following is a list of Diplomatic Missions to the United Nations and other international organizations based in Geneva (or responsible for affairs there). Where a specific member of a mission is named as having responsibility for WTO matters then their name is included in addition to that of the ambassador. Where a separate address from the main mission has been given for WTO affairs then that address alone is provided below.

AFGHANISTAN

Sherahmad NASRI
Ambassador

ADDRESS: Permanent mission of Afghanistan
              Rue de Lausanne 63
              5th Floor
              1202 Geneva
              Switzerland

TELEPHONE: + 41 22 731 16 16
FACSIMILE: + 41 22 731 45 10

ALBANIA

Andi GJONEJ
Ambassador

ADDRESS: Permanent mission of Albania

Rue du Môle 32 (Apt. 23)
1201 Geneva
Switzerland

TELEPHONE: + 41 22 731 11 43
FACSIMILE: + 41 22 738 81 56

ALGERIA

Hocine MEGHLAOUI
Ambassador

ADDRESS: Permanent mission of Algeria
Route de Lausanne 308
1293 Bellevue
Switzerland

TELEPHONE: + 41 22 774 19 85 - + 41 22 774 19 87
FACSIMILE: + 41 22 774 30 49

ANGOLA

Adriano A. TEIXEIRA PARREIRA
Ambassador extraordinary and plenipotentiary

ADDRESS: Permanent mission of Angola
Route de Chêne 109
1224 Chêne-Bougeries
Switzerland

TELEPHONE: + 41 22 348 40 50
FACSIMILE: + 41 22 348 40 46

ANTIGUA AND BARBUDA

James A. E. THOMAS, C. M. G.
Ambassador

ADDRESS: Permanent mission Antigua and Barbuda
15, Thayer Street

London W1M 5LD
United Kingdom

TELEPHONE: + 44 171 486 70 73
FACSIMILE: + 44 171 486 99 70

ARGENTINA

Juan Carlos SANCHEZ ARNAU
Ambassador extraordinary and plenipotentiary

ADDRESS: Permanent mission of Argentina
                Route de l'Aéroport 10
                Case Postale 536
                1215 Geneva 15
                Switzerland

TELEPHONE: + 41 22 798 19 52
FACSIMILE: + 41 22 798 59 95

ARMENIA

Achot MELIK-CHAHNAZARIAN
Ambassador

ADDRESS: Government House 1
                Square of the Republic
                Yerevan - 375010
                Armenia

TELEPHONE: + 7885 / 252 4332
FACSIMILE: + 7885 / 215 1069

AUSTRALIA

Penelope Anne WENSLEY
Ambassador

Donald KENYON
Ambassador (WTO)

111

ADDRESS: Permanent mission of Australia
             Rue de Moillebeau 56
             1209 Geneva
             Case Postale 172
             1211 Geneva 19
             Switzerland

TELEPHONE: + 41 22 918 29 00
FACSIMILE: + 41 22 733 65 86

AUSTRIA

Harald KREID
Ambassador

Johannes POTOCNIK
Minister (Economic affairs/WTO)

ADDRESS: Permanent mission of Austria
             Rue de Varembé 9-11
             Case Postale 68
             1211 Geneva 20
             Switzerland

TELEPHONE: + 41 22 733 77 50
FACSIMILE: + 41 22 740 05 04

BAHRAIN

Ahmed Mahdi AL-HADDAD
Ambassador

ADDRESS: Permanent mission of Bahrain
             Chemin William Barbey 51
             Case Postale 39
             1292 Chambésy
             Switzerland

TELEPHONE: + 41 22 758 21 02 - + 41 22 758 21 03
FACSIMILE: + 41 22 758 13 10

BANGLADESH

Anwar HASHIM
Ambassador

ADDRESS: Permanent mission of Bangladesh
             Rue de Lausanne 65
             1202 Geneva
             Switzerland

TELEPHONE: + 41 22 732 59 40 - + 41 22 732 59 49
FACSIMILE: + 41 22 738 46 16

BARBADOS

H. E. Mr Michael KING
Ambassador

ADDRESS: Embassy of Barbados
             Avenue Général Lartigue 78
             B-1200 Woluwe St. Lambert
             Belgium

TELEPHONE: + 41 22 732 17 37 - + 41 22 732 18 67
FACSIMILE: + 41 22 732 32 66

BELARUS

Stanislau S. AGURTSOU
Ambassador

ADDRESS: Permanent mission of Belarus
             Avenue de la Paix 15
             Case Postale
             1211 Geneva 20
             Switzerland

TELEPHONE: + 41 22 734 38 44
FACSIMILE: + 41 22 734 40 44

BELGIUM

Lodewijk WILLEMS
Ambassador extraordinary and plenipotentiary

John CORNET d'ELZIUS
First Secretary (WTO)

ADDRESS: Permanent mission of Belgium
             Rue de Moillebeau 58 (6th Floor)
             Case Postale 473
             1211 Geneva 19
             Switzerland

TELEPHONE: + 41 22 733 81 50
FACSIMILE: + 41 22 734 50 79

BELIZE

Jean TAMER
Ambassador

ADDRESS: Permanent mission of Belize
             International Center Cointrin (ICC)
             Route de Pré-Bois 20
             Case Postale 1906
             1215 Geneva 15
             Switzerland

TELEPHONE: + 41 22 788 21 07
FACSIMILE: + 41 22 788 21 15

BENIN

Edmond CAKPO-TOZO*
Ambassador extraordinary and plenipotentiary

ADDRESS: Permanent mission of Benin
             5, avenue de l'Observatoire
             B - 1180 Brussels
             Belgium

TELEPHONE: +32 2 374 91 92 - +32 2 375 06 74
FACSIMILE: +32 2 375 83 26

*   Residing in Brussels

BHUTAN

Jigmi Y. THINLEY
Ambassador extraordinary and plenipotentiary

ADDRESS: Permanent mission of Bhutan
              Chemin du Champ-d'Anier 17-19
              1209 Geneva
              Switzerland

TELEPHONE: +41 22 798 79 71
FACSIMILE: +41 22 788 25 93

BOLIVIA

Jorge Lema PATINO
Ambassador

ADDRESS: Permanent mission of Bolivia
              Rue du Valais 7 bis
              1202 Geneva
              Switzerland

TELEPHONE: +41 22 731 27 25 - +41 22 731 30 96
FACSIMILE: +41 22 738 00 22

BOSNIA-HERZEGOVINA

Mustafa BIJEDIC
Ambassador extraordinary and plenipotentiary
ADDRESS: Permanent mission of Bosnia-Herzegovina
              Rue Lamartine 22 bis
              1203 Geneva
              Switzerland

TELEPHONE: + 41 22 345 88 44 - + 41 22 345 88 58
FACSIMILE: + 41 22 345 88 89

BOTSWANA

ADDRESS: The Director
Department of Commerce and Comsumer Affairs
Ministry of Commerce and Industry
Private Bag 00252
Gaborone
Botswana

TELEPHONE: + 267 360 12 00
FACSIMILE: + 267 37 15 39

BRAZIL

Celso LAFER
Ambassador
Permanent assistant representative

ADDRESS: Permanent mission of Brazil
Ancienne Route 17B
1218 Grand-Saconnex
Switzerland

TELEPHONE: + 41 22 929 09 00
FACSIMILE: + 41 22 788 25 05 - + 41 22 788 25 06

BRUNEI DARUSSALAM

Mohd. Hamid Mohd. JAAFAR
Charge d'affaires a.i.

ADDRESS: Permanent mission of Brunei Darussalam
Avenue Blanc 46
1202 Geneva
Switzerland

TELEPHONE: + 41 22 738 11 44

FACSIMILE: + 41 22 738 23 16

BULGARIA

Valentin DOBREV
Ambassador

ADDRESS: Permanent mission of Bulgaria
Chemin des Crêts-de-Pregny 16
1218 Grand-Saconnex
Switzerland

TELEPHONE: + 41 22 798 03 00 - + 41 22 798 03 01
FACSIMILE: + 41 22 798 03 02

BURKINO FASO

S.E.M. Youssouf OUEDRAOGO
Ambassadeur, Représentant permanent auprès de l'OMC

ADDRESS: Ambassade de la République de Burkina Faso
Place Guy d'Arezzo 16
B-1060 Bruxelles
Belgium

TELEPHONE: + 41 22 345 99 12
FACSIMILE: + 41 22 235 06 12

BURUNDI

Appolonie SIMBIZI
Ambassador extraordinary and plenipotentiary

ADDRESS: Permanent mission of Burundi
Rue Fort-Barreau 13
1201 Geneva
Switzerland

TELEPHONE: + 41 22 740 29 19 - + 41 22 740 29 11
FACSIMILE: + 41 22 740 29 17

CAMBODIA

ADDRESS: Ministère du Commerce du
             Royaume du Camboge
             Boulevard Preah Norodom 20 - B
             Phnom Penh
             Cambodia

TELEPHONE: +855 232 63 96
FACSIMILE: +855 232 6396

CAMEROON

François-Xavier NGOUBEYOU
Ambassador

ADDRESS: Permanent mission of Cameroon
             Rue du Nant 6-8
             1207 Geneva
             Switzerland

TELEPHONE: +41 22 736 20 22
FACSIMILE: +41 22 736 21 65

CANADA

John WEEKES
Ambassador

Pierre GOSSELIN
Minister (Economic affairs)
Deputy representative

ADDRESS: Permanent mission of Canada
             Rue du Pré-de-la-Bichette 1
             1202 Geneva
             Switzerland

TELEPHONE: +41 22 919 92 00
FACSIMILE: +41 22 919 92 33

CAPE VERDE

Antonio RODRIGUES PIRES*
Ambassador extraordinary and plenipotentiary

ADDRESS: Permanent mission of Cape Verde
Ambassade de la République du Cap-Vert
113, Meckenheimer Allee
53115 Bonn 1
Germany

TELEPHONE: + 49 228 65 16 04 - + 49 228 69 55 13
FACSIMILE: + 49 228 63 05 88
* Residing in Bonn

CENTRAL AFRICAN REPUBLIC

ADDRESS: Ministere de l'Economie
Case Postale 736
Bangui
Central African Republic

FACSIMILE: + 236 61 36 00

CHAD

S.E.M. Ramadane BARMA
Ambassadeur

ADDRESS: Ambassade de la République du Tchad
Boulevard Lambermont 52
B-1030 Bruxelles
Belgium

TELEPHONE: + 322 215 19 75
FACSIMILE: + 322 216 35 26

CHILE

Carmen LUZ GUARDA

Ambassador

ADDRESS: Permanent mission of Chile
                Rue de Moillebeau 58 (4th Floor)
                Case Postale 110
                1211 Geneva 19
                Switzerland

TELEPHONE: + 41 22 734 51 30
FACSIMILE: + 41 22 734 41 94

CHINA

WU Jianmin
Ambassador

ADDRESS: Permanent mission of China
                Chemin de Surville 11
                1213 Petit-Lancy
                Switzerland

TELEPHONE: + 41 22 792 25 48 - + 41 22 793 70 13
FACSIMILE: + 41 22 793 70 14

COLOMBIA

Nestor Osorio LONDONO
Ambassador extraordinary and plenipotentiary

Nestor Osorio LONDONO
Ambassador
Permanent Representative to the WTO

ADDRESS: Permanent mission of Colombia to the WTO
                Avenue Giuseppe Motta 48 (6th Floor)
                1202 Geneva
                Switzerland

TELEPHONE: + 41 22 919 05 10 - + 41 22 919 05 14
FACSIMILE: + 41 22 734 60 94

CONGO

S.E.M. Paul Alexandre MAPINGU
Ambassadeur

ADDRESS: Ambassade de la République du Congo
             Avenue Franklin Roosevelt 16
             B-1050 Bruxelles
             Belgium

TELEPHONE: + 322 648 38 56
Facsimile: + 322 648 42 13

COSTA RICA

Manuel B. DENGO BENAVIDES
Ambassador

Ronald SABORIO SOTO
Ambassador, Permanent representative to the WTO

ADDRESS: Permanent mission of Costa Rica
             Rue de Butini 11
             1202 Geneva
             Switzerland

TELEPHONE: + 41 22 731 25 87
FACSIMILE: + 41 22 731 20 69

CROATIA

Miomir ZUZUL
Ambassador

ADDRESS: Permanent mission of Croatia
             Route de Ferney 25
             1209 Geneva
             Switzerland

TELEPHONE: + 41 22 740 32 43 - + 41 22 740 32 44
FACSIMILE: + 41 22 740 32 51

CUBA

Eumelio Caballero RODRIGUEZ
Ambassador
Arnaldo HERNANDEZ PEREZ
First Secretary (WTO)

ADDRESS: Permanent mission of Cuba
Chemin de Valérie 100
1292 Chambésy
Switzerland

TELEPHONE: + 41 22 758 23 26 - + 41 22 758 23 27
FACSIMILE: + 41 22 758 23 77

CYPRUS

Nicolaos D. MACRIS
Ambassador

ADDRESS: Permanent mission of Cyprus
Chemin François-Lehmann 34 (7th Floor)
Case Postale 113
1218 Grand-Saconnex
Switzerland

TELEPHONE: + 41 22 798 21 50 - + 41 22 798 21 75
FACSIMILE: + 41 22 791 00 84

CZECH REPUBLIC

Peter PALECKA

ADDRESS: Permanent mission of Czeck Republic
Chemin Louis Dunant 17
Case Postale 109
1211 Geneva 20
Switzerland

TELEPHONE: + 41 22 740 38 88 - + 41 22 740 36 68 - + 41 22 740 36 61
FACSIMILE: + 41 22 740 36 62

DENMARK

Jakob ESPER LARSEN
Ambassador

Vibeke ROOSEN
Counsellor Minister
Permanent assistant representative to the WTO

ADDRESS: Permanent mission of Denmark
Rue de Moillebeau 56 (7th Floor)
Case Postale 435
1211 Geneva 19
Switzerland

TELEPHONE: + 41 22 733 71 50
FACSIMILE: + 41 22 733 29 17

DJIBOUTI

M. Hassan DOUALEH
Représantant du Gouvernement de Djibouti aupres de l'OMC

ADDRESS: Rue Dentand 4
1202 Genevè
Switzerland

TELEPHONE: + 41 22 738 50 91

DOMINICA

Hugo LODRINI
Ambassador

ADDRESS: Permanent mission of Dominica
Avenue Eugène-Pittard 7
1206 Geneva
Switzerland

TELEPHONE: + 41 22 789 05 50 - + 41 22 789 04 42
FACSIMILE: + 41 22 789 18 66

DOMINICAN REPUBLIC

Angelina BONETTI HERRERA
Ambassador

Address: Permanent mission of Dominican Republic
Rue de Lausanne 65 (2nd Floor)
1202 Geneva
Switzerland

TELEPHONE: + 41 22 731 30 79
FACSIMILE: + 41 22 741 05 90

ECUADOR

Alfredo PINOARGOTE CEVALLOS
Ambassador

ADDRESS: Permanent mission of Ecuador
Rue de Lausanne 139 (6th Floor)
1202 Geneva
Switzerland

TELEPHONE: + 41 22 731 48 79 - + 41 22 731 52 89
FACSIMILE: + 41 22 738 26 76

EGYPT

Mounir ZAHRAN
Ambassador

ADDRESS: Permanent mission of Egypt
Avenue Blanc 49 (2nd Floor)
1202 Geneva
Switzerland

TELEPHONE: + 41 22 731 65 30 - + 41 22 731 65 39 - + 41 22 731 26 38
FACSIMILE: + 41 22 738 44 15

EL SALVADOR

Carlos Ernesto MENDOZA
Ambassador

Carmen TOBAR SANDOVAL
Counsellor Minister (WTO)

ADDRESS: Permanent mission of El Salvador
             Rue de Lausanne 65 (2nd Floor)
             1202 Geneva
             Switzerland

TELEPHONE: + 41 22 732 70 36 - + 41 22 732 75 77
FACSIMILE: + 41 22 738 47 44

ESTONIA

Mr Priit PALLUM
Chargé d'affaires a.i.

ADDRESS: Permanent Mission of Estonia to the United Nations
             Office at Geneva
             Chemin du Petit-Saconnex 28A
             1209 Geneva
             Switzerland

TELEPHONE: + 41 22 733 40 00
FACSIMILE: + 41 22 733 46 00

Postal
Address: Case postal 358
             1211 Genève 19

ETHIOPIA

Yousuff IBRAHIM OMAR
Ambassador

ADDRESS: Permanent mission of Ethiopia
             Rue de Moillebeau 56

125

Case Postale 338
1211 Geneva 19
Switzerland

TELEPHONE: + 41 22 733 07 50 - + 41 22 733 07 58 - + 41 22 733 07 59
FACSIMILE: + 41 22 740 11 29

EUROPEAN UNION

Jean-Pierre LENG
Ambassador
Permanent representative to the WTO

Hervé JOUANJEAN
Minister
Permanent representative to the WTO

ADDRESS: Permanent mission of the European Union
               Rue de Vermont 37-39
               Case Postale 195
               1211 Geneva 20
               Switzerland

TELEPHONE: + 41 22 918 22 11
FACSIMILE: + 41 22 734 22 36

FIJI

H.E. Mr Kalioate TAVOLA
Ambassador

ADDRESS: Embassy of the Republic of Fiji
               Avenue de Cortenberg 66, bte 7
               B-1000 Bruxelles
               Belgium

TELEPHONE: + 322 736 90 50
FACSIMILE: + 322 736 14 58

FINLAND

Björn EKBLOM
Counsellor Minister (WTO)

ADDRESS: Permanent mission of Finland
Rue Pré-de-la-Bichette 1
Case Postale 198
1211 Geneva 20
Switzerland

TELEPHONE: + 41 22 919 42 42
FACSIMILE: + 41 22 740 02 87

FRANCE

Michel de BONNECORSE
Ambassador

Jean-Marie METZGER
Counsellor Minister, Permanent representative to the WTO

ADDRESS: Permanent mission of France
Rue de Moillebeau 58
Case Postale 235
1211 Geneva 19
Switzerland

TELEPHONE: + 41 22 734 30 30
FACSIMILE: + 41 22 734 31 94

GABON

Emmanuel MBA ALLO
Ambassador

ADDRESS: Permanent mission of Gabon
Rue Henri Veyrassat 7 bis
Case Postale 12
1211 Geneva 7
Switzerland

127

TELEPHONE: + 41 22 345 80 01 - + 41 22 345 72 17
FACSIMILE: + 41 22 340 23 09

GAMBIA

Ruth A SOWE
Ambassador extraordinary and plenipotentiary

ADDRESS: Permanent mission of Gambia
Avenue Franklin D Roosevelt 126
B - 1050 Bruxelles
Belgium

TELEPHONE: + 32 2640 10 49
FACSIMILE: + 32 2646 32 77

GERMANY

Alois JELONEK
Ambassador

Peter WITT
Counsellor Minister (Commercial affairs/WTO)

ADDRESS: Permanent mission of Germany to the WTO
Chemin du Petit - Saconnex 28C
Case Postale 171
1211 Geneva 19
Switzerland

TELEPHONE: + 41 22 730 12 52/53
FACSIMILE: + 41 22 730 12 67

GHANA

Agnes AGGREY - ORLEANS
Ambassador

ADDRESS: Permanent mission of Ghana
Rue de Moillebeau 56

1209 Geneva
Switzerland

TELEPHONE: + 41 22 734 91 50
FACSIMILE: + 41 22 734 91 61

GREECE

Georges P. HELMIS
Ambassador

ADDRESS: Permanent mission of Greece
                Place Saint-Gervais 1
                1201 Geneva
                Switzerland

TELEPHONE: + 41 22 732 33 56 - + 41 22 732 33 57 - + 41 22 732 39 68
                + 41 22 732 38 25 (WTO) - + 41 22 732 36 48 (WTO)
FACSIMILE: + 41 22 732 21 50

GRENADA

Mr Samuel ORGIAS
Minister-Counsellor
Acting Permanent Representative to the WTO

ADDRESS: Mission of Grenada to the EEC
                Avenue de la Toison d'Or 24
                B-1060 Bruxelles
                Belgium

TELEPHONE: + 32 2 514 12 42
FACSIMILE: + 32 2 513 87 24

GUATEMALA

Federico URRUELA PRADO
Ambassador

ADDRESS: Permanent mission of Guatemala

Chemin de Sous-Bois 21
1202 Geneva
Switzerland

TELEPHONE: + 41 22 734 55 73 - + 41 22 733 08 50
FACSIMILE: + 41 22 733 14 29

GUINEA

ADDRESS: Permanent mission of Guinea
               Ambassade de la République de Guinée
               BP 1210
               Conakry
               Switzerland

TELEPHONE: + 41 22 44 22 39
FACSIMILE: + 41 22 41 11 19

GUINEA BISSAU

Fali EMBALO
Ambassador

ADDRESS: Permanent mission of Guinea Bissau
               Ambassade de la République de Guinea Bissau
               70, avenue Franklin Roosevelt
               B-1050 Brussels
               Belgium

TELEPHONE: + 32 2 647 08 90 - + 32 2 647 13 51
FACSIMILE: + 32 2 640 43 12

EQUATORIAL GUINEA

Pedro EDJANG MBA MEDJA*
Ambassador extraordinary and plenipotentiary

ADDRESS: Permanent mission of Equatorial Guinea
               Ambassade de la République de Guinée équatoriale
               6, rue Alfred de Vigny

75008 Paris
France

TELEPHONE:	+ 33 1 47 66 44 33
FACSIMILE:	+ 33 1 47 64 94 52

* Residing in Paris

GUYANA

H.E. Mr Laleshwar K.N. SINGH
High Commissioner for the Co-operative Republic of Guyana

ADDRESS:	Guyana High Commission
	Palace Court 3
	Bayswater Road
	London W2 4LP

TELEPHONE:	+ 44 71 229 7684
FACSIMILE:	+ 44 71 727 9809

HAITI

Joseph Philippe ANTONIO
Ambassador

ADDRESS:	Permanent mission of Haiti
	Rue de Monthoux 64
	1201 Geneva
	Switzerland

TELEPHONE:	+ 41 22 732 76 28
FACSIMILE:	+ 41 22 732 55 36

HONDURAS

Arturo Guillermo LOPEZ LUNA
Ambassador extraordinary and plenipotentiary

Carlos H. MATUTE IRIAS*
Ambassador
Permanent Representative to the WTO

*ADDRESS: Permanent mission of Honduras
                Rue du Cendrier 15 (3rd Floor)
                1201 Geneva
                Switzerland

TELEPHONE: + 41 22 741 05 05 - + 41 22 741 05 07
FACSIMILE: + 41 22 741 05 08

HONG KONG

Stuart W. HARBINSON
Permanent Representative of Hong Kong to the WTO

Miss Annie H.Y. TANG
Deputy Representative

ADDRESS: Hong Kong Economic and Trade Office
                Rue de Vermont 37-39
                1202 Genève
                Switzerland

Postal   Case Postale 95
Address: 1211 Genève 20

TELEPHONE: + 41 22 734 90 40
TELEFAX: + 41 22 733 99 04 - + 41 22 740 15 01

HUNGARY

György BOYTHA
Ambassador extraordinary and plenipotentiary

András LAKATOS
Ambassador extraordinary and plenipotentiary
Permanent Representative to the WTO

*ADDRESS: Permanent mission of Hungary
                Rue de Lausanne 80
                1202 Geneva
                Switzerland

TELEPHONE: + 41 22 731 74 84 - + 41 22 731 51 36
FACSIMILE: + 41 22 738 46 09

ICELAND

Gunnar Snorri GUNNARSSON
Ambassador extraordinary and plenipotentiary

ADDRESS: Permanent mission of Iceland
              Rue de Varembé 9-11
              Case Postale 86
              1211 Geneva 20
              Switzerland

TELEPHONE: + 41 22 733 96 87 - + 41 22 734 02 28
FACSIMILE: + 41 22 733 28 39

INDIA

Satish CHANDRA
Ambassador

Srinivasan NARAYANAN*
Ambassador
Permanent Representative to the WTO

*ADDRESS: Permanent mission of India
              Rue du Valais 9 (6th Floor)
              1201 Geneva
              Switzerland

TELEPHONE: + 41 22 738 44 43 - + 41 22 738 44 72
FACSIMILE: + 41 22 738 45 48

INDONESIA

Agus TARMIDZI
Ambassador extraordinary and plenipotentiary

ADDRESS: Permanent mission of Indonesia

Rue de Saint-Jean 16
Case Postale 2271
1211 Geneva 2
Switzerland

TELEPHONE: + 41 22 345 33 50 - + 41 22 345 33 57 - + 41 22 345 33 59
FACSIMILE: + 41 22 345 57 33

IRAN

Sirous NASSERI
Ambassador

ADDRESS: Permanent mission of Iran
Chemin du Petit-Saconnex 28
1209 Geneva
Switzerland

TELEPHONE: + 41 22 733 30 01 - + 41 22 733 30 04
FACSIMILE: + 41 22 733 02 03

IRAQ

Barzan Ibrahim AL-TIKRITI
Ambassador

ADDRESS: Permanent mission of Irak
Chemin du Petit-Saconnex 28a
1209 Geneva
Switzerland

TELEPHONE: + 41 22 734 07 60
FACSIMILE: + 41 22 733 03 26

IRELAND

Anne ANDERSON
Ambassador

P FANNING

First Secretary (WTO)

ADDRESS: Permanent mission of Ireland
Rue de Lausanne 45-47
Case Postale 2566
1211 Geneva 2
Switzerland

TELEPHONE: + 41 22 732 85 50
FACSIMILE: + 41 22 732 81 06 - + 41 22 731 43 65

ISRAEL

Yoseph LAMDAN
Ambassador extraordinary and plenipotentiary

Raphaël WALDEN
Counsellor Minister
Permanent representative to the WTO

ADDRESS: Permanent mission of Israel
Chemin Bonvent 9
1216 Cointrin
Switzerland

TELEPHONE: + 41 22 798 05 00
FACSIMILE: + 41 22 798 49 50

ITALY

Giuseppe BALDOCCI
Ambassador

ADDRESS: Permanent mission of Italy
Chemin de l'Impératrice 10
1292 Chambésy
Switzerland

TELEPHONE: + 41 22 918 08 10
FACSIMILE: + 41 22 910 17 12

IVORY COAST

Koffi KOUAME
Ambassador

ADDRESS: Permanent mission of Ivory Coast
Avenue Blanc 47
Case Postale 76
1211 Geneva 21
Switzerland

TELEPHONE: +41 22 731 89 60 - +41 22 731 89 68 - +41 22 731 89 69

FACSIMILE: +41 22 731 93 38

JAMAICA

K G Antony HILL
Ambassador extraordinary and plenipotentiary

ADDRESS: Permanent mission of Jamaica
Rue de Lausanne 36
1201 Geneva
Switzerland

TELEPHONE: +41 22 731 57 80 - +41 22 731 57 89
FACSIMILE: +41 22 738 44 20

JAPAN

Minoru ENDO
Ambassador

ADDRESS: Permanent mission of Japan
Chemin des Fins 3
Case Postale 337
1211 Geneva 19
Switzerland

TELEPHONE: +41 22 717 31 11 - +41 22 717 34 44
FACSIMILE: +41 22 788 38 11

JORDAN

Abdullah MADADHA
Ambassador

ADDRESS: Permanent mission of Jordan
             Rue de Lausanne 45-47
             Case Postale 1716
             1211 Geneva 1
             Switzerland

TELEPHONE: + 41 22 731 71 34
FACSIMILE: + 41 22 738 58 41

KAZAKHSTAN

Mrs Z YERTLESSOVA
First Deputy Minister of Economy

ADDRESS: Ministry of Economy
             115 Zheltoksan
             480095 Almaty
             Kazakhstan

TELEPHONE: 7 3272 - 69 51 43
FACSIMILE: 7 3272 - 63 66 05

KENYA

Esther M TOLLE
Ambassador

ADDRESS: Permanent mission of Kenya
             Chemin des Mines 2
             1202 Geneva
             Switzerland

TELEPHONE: + 41 22 732 72 72 - + 41 22 732 70 38
FACSIMILE: + 41 22 731 29 05

NORTH KOREA

RI Tcheul
Ambassador

ADDRESS: Permanent mission of North Korea
Chemin de Plonjon 1
1207 Geneva
Switzerland

TELEPHONE: + 41 22 735 43 70
FACSIMILE: + 41 22 786 06 62

SOUTH KOREA

JOUN Yung Sun
Ambassador

ADDRESS: Permanent mission of South Korea
Route de Pré-Bois 20
Case Postale 566
1215 Geneva 15
Switzerland

TELEPHONE: + 41 22 791 01 11
FACSIMILE: + 41 22 788 62 49

KUWAIT

Mohammad S. AL-SALLAL
Ambassador

ADDRESS: Permanent mission of Kuwait
Avenue de l'Ariana 2
1202 Geneva
Switzerland

TELEPHONE: + 41 22 734 96 00
FACSIMILE: + 41 22 740 21 55

LATVIA

Sandra KALNIETE
Ambassador
Indulis ABELIS
Third Secretary (WTO)

ADDRESS: Permanent mission of Latvia
Case Postale 193
1211 Geneva 20
Switzerland

TELEPHONE: +41 22 738 51 11
FACSIMILE: +41 22 738 51 71

LEBANON

Cheikh Amine EL KHAZEN
Ambassador

ADDRESS: Permanent mission of Lebanon
Avenue de Budé 10 (6th Floor)
1202 Geneva
Switzerland

TELEPHONE: +41 22 733 81 40 - +41 22 733 81 49
FACSIMILE: +41 22 740 11 66

LESOTHO

Potlako NZIMA - NTSEKHE
Ambassador

ADDRESS: Permanent mission of Lesotho
Ambassade du Royaume du Lesotho
45, boulevard Général Wahis
B-1030 Brussels
Belgium

TELEPHONE: +32 2 736 39 76 - +32 2 736 67 70
FACSIMILE: +32 2 734 67 70

LIBERIA

ADDRESS: Permanent mission of Liberia
Rue du Valais 9
1202 Geneva
Switzerland

TELEPHONE: + 41 22 731 25 83
FACSIMILE: + 41 22 27 190

LIBYA

ADDRESS: Permanent mission of Libya
Avenue Blanc 47
1202 Geneva
Switzerland

TELEPHONE: + 41 22 731 82 04 - + 41 22 731 82 05
FACSIMILE: + 41 22 732 88 19

LIECHTENSTEIN

ADDRESS: Office for Foreign Affairs
Heiligkruez 14
9490 Vaduz
Lichtenstein

TELEPHONE: + 41 75 236 6058
FACSIMILE: + 41 75 236 60 59

LITHUANIA

Narcizas PRIELAIDA
Ambassador extraordinary and plenipotentiary

ADDRESS: Permanent mission of Lithuania
Château-Banquet 20
1202 Geneva
Switzerland

TELEPHONE: +41 22 731 55 20 - +41 22 731 50 65
FACSIMILE: +41 22 731 55 20

LUXEMBOURG

Jacques REUTER
Ambassador

ADDRESS: Permanent mission of Luxembourg
              Chemin du Petit-Saconnex 28A
              1209 Geneva
              Switzerland

TELEPHONE: +41 22 734 33 80 - +41 22 734 33 89
FACSIMILE: +41 22 733 09 96 - +41 22 733 95 86

MACAU

Alexandra Costa GOMES
Permanent Representative to the WTO

ADDRESS: Delegation of Macau
              Avenue Louise 375, bte 9
              B-1050 Bruxelles
              Belgium

TELEPHONE: +32 2 647 12 65
FACSIMILE: +32 2 640 15 52

FORMER YUGOSLAV REPUBLIC OF MACEDONIA

Goce PETRESKI
Ambassador extraordinary and plenipotentiary

ADDRESS: Permanent mission of former
              Yugoslav Republic of Macedonia
              Rue de Lausanne 143, 6th Floor, No. 64
              1202 Geneva
              Switzerland

TELEPHONE: + 41 22 731 29 30
FACSIMILE: + 41 22 731 29 39

MADAGASCAR

Jaona RAVALOSON
Ambassador extraordinary and plenipotentiary

ADDRESS: Permanent mission of Madagascar
Avenue Riant-Parc 32
1209 Geneva
Switzerland

TELEPHONE: + 41 22 740 16 50
FACSIMILE: + 41 22 740 16 16

MALAWI

H.E. Mr G.C. CHIPUNGU
Ambassador

ADDRESS: Embassy of the Republic of Malawi
Mainzer Strasse 124
D-53179 Bonn
Germany

TELEPHONE: + 49 228 34 30 16 - + 49 228 34 30 19
FACSIMILE: + 49 228 34 06 19

MALAYSIA

HARON Siraj
Ambassador

ADDRESS: Permanent mission of Malaysia
International Cointrin Centre
Bat. H - 1er étage
Route de Pré-Bois 20
Case Postale 711
1215 Geneva 15

Switzerland

TELEPHONE: +41 22 788 15 05 - +41 22 788 15 09 - +41 22 788 15 23
FACSIMILE: +41 22 788 04 92 - +41 22 788 09 75

MALDIVES

ADDRESS: Ministry of Trade and Industries of the Republic of
Maldives
Ghazee Building
Ameeru Ahmed Magu
20-05 Malé
Maldives
TELEPHONE: +360 32 36 68 - +360 32 38 40
FACSIMILE: +360 32 37 56

MALI

Ousmane DEMBELE
Ambassador extraordinary and plenipotentiary

ADDRESS: Permanent mission of Mali
Ambassade de la République du Mali
Basteistrasse 86
D - 53179 Bonn
Germany

TELEPHONE: +49 228 35 70 48
FACSIMILE: +49 228 36 19 22

MALTA

Michael BARTOLO
Ambassador

ADDRESS: Permanent mission of Malta
Parc du Château-Banquet 26
1202 Geneva
Switzerland

TELEPHONE: + 41 22 901 05 80
FACSIMILE: + 41 22 738 11 20

MAURITANIA

S.E.M. Ahmed Ould Sid' AHMED
Ambassadeur

ADDRESS: Ambassade de la Républic islamique de Mauritanie
             Avenue de la Colombie 6
             B-1050 Bruxelles
             Belgium

TELEPHONE: + 32 2 672 47 47
FACSIMILE: + 32 2 672 30 51

MAURITIUS

Patrice E CURÉ
Minister Counsellor

ADDRESS: Permanent mission of Mauritius
             Chemin Louis-Dunant 7-9
             1202 Geneva
             Switzerland

TELEPHONE: + 41 22 734 85 50
FACSIMILE: + 41 22 86 30

MEXICO

Alejandro de la PENA
Ambassador

ADDRESS: Permanent mission of Mexico
             Avenue de Budé 10A
             1202 Geneva
             Switzerland

TELEPHONE: + 41 22 734 30 31

FACSIMILE: +41 22 733 14 15

MOLDOVA

H.E. Mr A CHEPTINE
Minister for Foreign Economic Relations

ADDRESS: Piata Marii Adunari Nationale 1
               277033 Kishinev
               Moldova

TELEPHONE: +37 32 22 11 33
FACSIMILE: +37 32 23 20 61

MONGOLIA

Shirchinjavyn YUMJAV
Ambassador

ADDRESS: Permanent mission of Mongolia
               Chemin des Mollies 4
               1293 Bellevue
               Switzerland

TELEPHONE: +41 22 774 19 74 - +41 22 774 19 75
FACSIMILE: +41 22 774 32 01

MOROCCO

Mohamed Nacer BENDJELLOUN-TOUIMI
Ambassador

Abdelkader LECHEHEB
Counsellor
Permanent representative to the WTO

ADDRESS: Permanent mission of Morocco
               Chemin François-Lehmann 18A
               Case Postale 244
               1218 Grand-Saconnex

Switzerland

TELEPHONE: + 41 22 798 15 35 - + 41 22 798 15 36
FACSIMILE: + 41 22 798 47 02

MOZAMBIQUE

ADDRESS: Permanent mission of Mozambique
Consulat général honoraire de la
République du Mozambique
Caixa Postal 1831
Maputo
Mozambique

TELEPHONE: + 258 42 72 04
FACSIMILE: + 258 43 12 06

MYANMAR

H. E. U. AYE
Ambassador extraordinary and plenipotentiary

ADDRESS: Permanent mission of Myanmar
Avenue Blanc 47
1202 Geneva
Switzerland

TELEPHONE: + 41 22 731 75 40
FACSIMILE: + 41 22 738 48 82

NAMIBIA

Dr. Zedekia J. NGAVIRUE
Ambassador

ADDRESS: Embassy of the Republic of Namibia
Avenue de Tervuren 454
B-1050 Bruxelles
Belgium

TELEPHONE:	+32 2 771 14 10
FACSIMILE:	+32 2 771 96 89

NEPAL

Bamali Prasad LACOUL
Minister - Counsellor

ADDRESS: Permanent mission of Nepal
Rue Frédéric Amiel 1
1203 Geneva
Switzerland

TELEPHONE:	+41 22 344 44 41 - +41 22 345 29 34
FACSIMILE:	+41 22 344 40 93

THE NETHERLANDS

Tiddo P. HOFSTEE
Ambassador
Anne-Marie PLATE
Counsellor
Permanent Representative to the WTO

ADDRESS: Permanent mission of The Netherlands
Chemin des Anémones 11
Case Postale 276
1219 Châtelaine
Switzerland

TELEPHONE:	+41 797 50 30
FACSIMILE:	+41 797 51 29

NEW ZEALAND

Wade ARMSTRONG
Ambassador

Martin HARVEY
Permanent Representative to the WTO

ADDRESS: Permanent mission of New Zealand
              Chemin du Petit-Saconnex 28a
              Case Postale 334
              1211 Geneva 19
              Switzerland

TELEPHONE: + 41 22 734 95 30
FACSIMILE: + 41 22 734 30 62

NICARAGUA

Lester MEJIA SOLIS
Ambassador

ADDRESS: Permanent mission of Nicaragua
              Rue du Roveray 16
              1207 Geneva
              Switzerland

TELEPHONE: + 41 22 736 66 44 - + 41 22 736 67 07
FACSIMILE: + 41 22 736 60 12

NIGER

Almoumine BAZINORE
Conseiller

ADDRESS: Permanent mission of Niger
              Chacellerie diplomatique
              78, avenue Franklin Roosevelt
              B-1050 Brussels
              Belgium

TELEPHONE: + 32 2 648 61 40
FACSIMILE: + 32 2 648 27 84

NIGERIA

Ejoh ABUAH
Ambassador

ADDRESS: Permanent mission of Nigeria
            Rue Richard Wagner 1
            1211 Geneva 2
            Switzerland

TELEPHONE: + 41 22 734 21 40 - + 41 22 734 21 49
FACSIMILE: + 41 22 734 10 53

NORWAY

Terje JOHANNESSEN, *Ambassador*

Ole LUNDBY, *Counsellor (WTO)*

ADDRESS: Permanent mission of Norway
            Avenue de Budé 35
            Case Postale 274
            1211 Geneva 19
            Switzerland

TELEPHONE: + 41 22 734 97 30
FACSIMILE: + 41 22 733 99 79

OMAN

Mohammed Omar Ahmed AIDEED
Ambassador extraordinary and plenipotentiary

ADDRESS: Permanent mission of Oman
            Chemin du Petit-Saconnex 28b (entrée C)
            1209 Geneva
            Switzerland

TELEPHONE: + 41 22 733 73 20
FACSIMILE: + 41 22 740 10 75

PAKISTAN

Munir AKRAM
Ambassador

ADDRESS: Permanent mission of Pakistan
            Rue de Moillebeau 56
            Case Postale 434
            1211 Geneva 19
            Switzerland

TELEPHONE: + 41 22 734 77 60
FACSIMILE: + 41 22 734 80 85

PANAMA

Yavel Francis LANUZA
Ambassador extraordinary and plenipotentiary

ADDRESS: Permanent mission of Panama
            Rue de Lausanne 72
            1202 Geneva
            Switzerland

TELEPHONE: + 41 22 738 03 88
FACSIMILE: + 41 22 738 03 63

PAPUA NEW GUINEA

Peter S. TSIAMALILI
Ambassador

ADDRESS: Embassy of Papua New Guinea
            Avenue de Tervuen 430
            B-1150 Bruxelles
            Belgium

TELEPHONE: + 322 779 08 26 - + 322 779 06 09
FACSIMILE: + 322 772 70 88 - + 322 772 59 12

PARAGUAY

Eladio LOIZAGA
Ambassador

ADDRESS: Permanent mission of Paraguay
                  Chemin du Petit - Saconnex 28A
                  1209 Geneva

TELEPHONE: + 41 22 740 32 11 - + 41 22 740 32 13
FACSIMILE: + 41 22 740 32 90

PERU

José URRUTIA
Ambassador

ADDRESS: Permanent mission of Peru
                  Rue de Lausanne 63 (6th Floor)
                  1202 Geneva
                  Switzerland

TELEPHONE: + 41 22 731 11 30 - + 41 22 731 11 39
FACSIMILE: + 41 22 731 11 68

PHILIPPINES

Lilia R. BAUTISTA
Ambassador

ADDRESS: Permanent mission of Philippines
                  Avenue Blanc 47
                  1202 Geneva
                  Switzerland

TELEPHONE: + 41 22 731 83 20 - + 41 22 731 83 29
FACSIMILE: + 41 22 731 68 88

POLAND

Ludwik DEMBINSKI
Ambassador

Jan MICHALEK
Counsellor Minister

Permanent Representative to the WTO

ADDRESS: Permanent mission of Poland
Chemin de l'Ancienne Route 15
Case Postale 126
1218 Grand-Saconnex
Switzerland

TELEPHONE: + 41 22 798 11 61
FACSIMILE: + 41 22 798 11 75

PORTUGAL

Gonçalo de SANTA CLARA GOMES
Ambassador

Isabel Maria MARQUEZ RIBEIRO DA SILVA
First Secretary (WTO)

ADDRESS: Permanent mission of Portugal
Rue Antoine Casteret 33
Case Postale 51
1211 Geneva 20
Switzerland

TELEPHONE: + 41 22 918 02 00
FACSIMILE: + 41 22 918 02 28

QATAR

Sheikh Fahad Awaida AL-THANI
Ambassador extraordinary and plenipotentiary

ADDRESS: Permanent mission of Qatar
Route de Ferney 149 b
1218 Grand-Saconnex
Switzerland

TELEPHONE: + 41 22 798 85 00 - + 41 22 798 85 01
FACSIMILE: + 41 22 791 04 85

ROMANIA

Romulus NEAGU
Ambassador

Adrian CONSTANTINESCU
Counsellor Minister
Permanent Representative to the WTO

Mihai BERINDE
Counsellor Minister
Permanent Representative to the WTO

ADDRESS: Permanent mission of Romania
               Chemin de la Perrière 6
               1223 Cologny
               Switzerland

TELEPHONE: +41 22 752 10 90 - +41 22 752 55 55
FACSIMILE: +41 22 752 29 76

RUSSIAN FEDERATION

Andrei KOLOSSOVSKY
Ambassador extraordinary and plenipotentiary

Vladimir KHREBTOV
Counsellor (Commercial affairs, WTO)

ADDRESS: Permanent mission of the Russian Federation
               Avenue de la Paix 15
               Case Postale
               1211 Geneva 20
               Switzerland

TELEPHONE: +41 22 733 18 70 - +41 22 734 66 30 - +41 22 734 46 18

FACSIMILE: +41 22 734 40 44

RWANDA

Jean-Marie Vianney MBONIMPA
Ambassadeur

ADDRESS: Permanent mission of Rwanda
Ambassade de la République rwandaise
Eigersrasse 60
3007 Berne
Switzerland

TELEPHONE: + 41 31 301 06 11
FACSIMILE: + 41 31 302 48 60

SAINT LUCIA

Edwin LAURENT
Ambassador

ADDRESS: Permanent Representative of Saint Lucia to the WTO
Rue des Aduatiques 100
B-1040 Bruxelles
Belgium

TELEPHONE: + 322 733 43 28 - + 41 22 733 54 82 - + 41 22 735 75 38
FACSIMILE: + 322 735 72 37

SAINT KITTS AND NEVIS

Aubrey HART
High Commissioner

ADDRESS: Permanent Representative to the WTO
High Commission for Eastern Caribbean States
10 Kensington Court
London W8 5DL

TELEPHONE: + 44 71 937 9522
FACSIMILE: + 44 71 937 5514

SAINT VINCENT AND THE GRENADINES

ADDRESS: Ministry of Foreign Affairs and Tourism
Kingstown

TELEPHONE: + 1 909 456 20 60
FACSIMILE: + 1 809 456 26 10

SAN MARINO

Dieter THOMAS
Ambassador

ADDRESS: Permanent mission of San Marino
Chemin Gilbert Trolliet 3
1209 Geneva
Switzerland

TELEPHONE: + 41 22 740 12 31
FACSIMILE: + 41 22 740 12 39

SAUDI ARABIA

Cheikh Ahmed ABDUL-JABBAR
Ambassador
Mussad M. S. AL-ESHAWI*
Attaché (WTO)

ADDRESS: Permanent mission of Saudi Arabia
Route de Lausanne 263
1292 Chambésy
Switzerland

TELEPHONE: + 41 22 758 24 41
FACSIMILE: + 41 22 738 41 28

*ADDRESS: Office of the Commercial Attaché (WTO)
Avenue Blanc 46
1202 Geneva
Switzerland

TELEPHONE: + 41 22 738 30 30

155

SENEGAL

Ibra Déguène KA
Ambassador extraordinary and plenipotentiary

ADDRESS: Permanent mission of Senegal
                Rue de la Servette 93
                1202 Geneva
                Switzerland

TELEPHONE: + 41 22 734 53 00
FACSIMILE: + 41 22 740 07 11

SEYCHELLES

ADDRESS: Ministry of Finance and Communications
                Trade and Commerce Division
                Central Bank Building
                Independent Avenue
                P.O. Box 313
                Victoria
                Mahé Island
                Seychelles

TELEPHONE: + 248 22 52 52
FACSIMILE: + 248 22 49 85

SIERRA LEONE

Alhaji S.B. TIMBO
Ambassador

ADDRESS: Embassy of the Republic of Sierra Leone
                Avenue de Tervuren 410
                B-1150 Bruxelles
                Belgium

TELEPHONE: + 32 2 771 00 53
FACSIMILE: + 32 2 7771 11 80

SINGAPORE

K. KESAVAPANY
Ambassador

ADDRESS: Permanent mission of Singapore
             Route de Pré-Bois 20
             Case Postale 1910
             1215 Geneva 15
             Switzerland

TELEPHONE: + 41 22 929 66 55
FACSIMILE: + 41 22 929 66 58

SLOVAK REPUBLIC

Mária KRASNOHORSKA
Ambassador extraordinary and plenipotentiary
Peter BRNO
Counsellor
Permanent Representative (Economic affairs/WTO)

ADDRESS: Permanent mission of the Slovak Republic
             Chemin de l'Ancienne route 9
             Case Postale 160
             1218 Grand-Saconnex
             Switzerland

TELEPHONE: + 41 22 798 91 81 - + 41 22 798 91 82
FACSIMILE: + 41 22 788 09 19

SLOVENIA

Anton Alex BEBLER
Ambassador

ADDRESS: Permanent mission of Slovenia
             Rue de Lausanne 147
             1202 Geneva
             Switzerland

TELEPHONE: +41 22 738 66 60
FACSIMILE: +41 22 738 66 65

SOLOMON ISLANDS

ADDRESS: The Director
               Trade Division
               Ministry of Commerce and Primary Industries
               P.O. Box G26
               Honiara
               Solomon Islands

TELEPHONE: +677 2 18 49
FACSIMILE: +677 2 16 51

SOMALI REPUBLIC

ADDRESS: Permanent mission of the Somali Republic
               Rue du Valais 9
               1202 Geneva
               Switzerland

TELEPHONE: +41 22 731 54 50
FACSIMILE: +41 22 798 07 32

SOUTH AFRICA

J S SELEBI
Ambassador

ADDRESS: Permanent mission of South Africa
               Rue du Rhône 65
               1204 Geneva
               Switzerland

TELEPHONE: +41 22 849 54 50
FACSIMILE: +41 22 849 54 00

SPAIN

Raimundo Pérez - Hernández y Torra
Ambassador

ADDRESS: Permanent mission of Spain
Avenue Blanc 53
1202 Geneva
Case Postale 201
1211 Geneva 20
Switzerland

TELEPHONE: + 41 22 731 22 30 - + 41 22 731 22 39
FACSIMILE: + 41 22 731 53 70

SRI LANKA

N. R. MEEMEDUMA
Ambassador

ADDRESS: Permanent mission of Sri Lanka
Rue de Moillebeau 56
Case Postale 436
1211 Geneva 19
Switzerland

TELEPHONE: + 41 22 734 93 40 - + 41 22 734 93 49
FACSIMILE: + 41 22 734 90 84

SUDAN

Ali Ahmed Sahloul
Ambassador

ADDRESS: Permanent mission of Sudan
Rue de Moillebeau 56
Case Postale 335
1211 Geneva 19
Switzerland

TELEPHONE: + 41 22 733 25 60 - + 41 22 733 25 68 - + 41 22 733 25 69

159

FACSIMILE: + 41 22 734 48 87

SURINAM

Ewald C. LEEFLANG
Ambassador

ADDRESS: Embassy of the Republic of Suriname
               Avenue Loiuse 379, bte 20
               B-1050 Bruxelles
               Belgium

TELEPHONE: + 32 2 640 11 72
FACSIMLIE: + 32 2 646 39 62

SWAZILAND

ADDRESS: The Principal Secretary
               Ministry of Commerce and Industry of Swaziland
               P.O. Box 451
               Mbabane
               Swaziland

TELEPHONE: + 268 - 43 201
TELEFAX: + 268 - 44 711

SWEDEN

Lars NORBERG
Ambassador
Christer MANHUSEN
Ambassador
Permanent Representative to the WTO

ADDRESS: Permanent mission of Sweden
               Rue de Lausanne 82
               1202 Geneva
               Case Postale 190
               1211 Geneva 20
               Switzerland

TELEPHONE: + 41 22 908 08 00
FACSIMILE: + 41 22 908 08 10

SWITZERLAND

William ROSSIER
Ambassador extraordinary and plenipotentiary
Head of the Mission to the WTO

ADDRESS: Permanent mission of Switzerland
               Rue de Varembé 9-11, 5th Floor
               Case Postale 107
               1211 Geneva 20
               Switzerland

TELEPHONE: + 41 22 749 25 25
FACSIMILE: + 41 22 734 56 23

SYRIA

ADDRESS: Permanent mission of Syria
               Rue de Lausanne 72 (3rd Floor)
               1202 Geneva
               Switzerland

TELEPHONE: + 41 22 732 65 22 - + 41 22 732 66 26
FACSIMILE: + 41 22 738 42 75

CHINESE TAIPEI

Steve Ruey-Long CHEN
Representative of the Seperate Customs Territory of Taiwan, Penghu,
Kinmen and Matsu to the WTO

ADDRESS: ICC Bloc G, 2ème étage
               Route de Pré-Bois 20
               1216 Cointrin
               Switzerland

TELEPHONE: + 41 22 788 65 80

FACSIMILE: + 41 22 788 65 82

Postal   Case Postale 1813
Address: 1215 Genène 15
               Switzerland

TANZANIA

Elly Elikunda Elineema MTANGO
Ambassador

ADDRESS: Permanent mission of Tanzania
               Avenue Blanc 47
               1202 Geneva
               Switzerland

TELEPHONE: + 41 22 731 89 20
FACSIMILE: + 41 22 732 82 55

THAILAND

D TULALAMBA
Ambassador

ADDRESS: Permanent mission of Thailand
               Route de Prés - Bois 20/5
               Case Postale 1848
               1215 Geneva 15
               Switzerland

TELEPHONE: + 41 22 929 52 00 - + 41 22 788 80 25
FACSIMILE: + 41 22 791 01 66

TOGO

Bitokotipou YAGNINIM
Ambassador

ADDRESS: Permanent mission of Togo
               1, rue Miollis

F - 75732 Paris Cédex 15
France

TELEPHONE: + 33 1 45 68 34 90
FACSIMILE: + 33 1 42 19 01 22

TONGA

ADDRESS: Secretary for Labour, Commerce and Industries of the
Kingdom of Tonga
P.O. Box 110
Nuku' Alofa
Tonga

TELEPHONE: + 676 23 688
TELEFAX: + 676 23 887

TRINIDAD & TOBAGO

Trevor C. Spencer
Ambassador extraordinary and plenipotentiary

ADDRESS: Permanent mission of Trinidad and Tobago
Rue de Vermont 35-39
1202 Geneva
Switzerland

TELEPHONE: + 41 22 918 03 80
FACSIMILE: + 41 22 734 91 38

TUNISIA

Mohamed ENNACEUR
Ambassador

ADDRESS: Permanent mission of Tunisia
Rue de Moillebeau 58
Case Postale 272
1211 Geneva 19
Switzerland

TELEPHONE: + 41 22 734 84 50 - + 41 22 734 84 59
FACSIMILE: + 41 22 734 06 63

TURKEY

Tugay ULUÇEVIK
Ambassador

ADDRESS: Permanent mission of Turkey
Chemin du Petit-Saconnex 28B
Case Postale 271
1211 Geneva 19
Switzerland

TELEPHONE: + 41 22 734 39 38 - + 41 22 734 39 39
FACSIMILE: + 41 22 734 08 59 - + 41 22 734 52 09

UGANDA

Kakima NTAMBI*
Ambassador extraordinary and plenipotentiary

ADDRESS: Permanent mission of Uganda
Ambassade de la République de l'Ouganda
317, avenue de Tervueren
B-1150 Brussels
Belgium

TELEPHONE: + 32 2 762 58 25
FACSIMILE: + 32 2 763 04 38
* Residing in Brussels

UKRAINE

Sergiy OSYKA
Minister for Foreign Economic Relations

ADDRESS: Ministry of Foreign Economic Relations
Lvovskaya Sq. 8
Kyiv GSP-655, 254 655

Ukraine

TELEPHONE: 380 56 212 39 85 - 380 56 212 15 78
FACSIMILE: 380 56 212 53 76 - 380 56 212 18 98

UNITED ARAB EMIRATES

Nasser Salman AL ABOODI
Ambassador extraordinary and plenipotentiary

ADDRESS: Permanent mission of United Arab Emirates
Rue de Moillebeau 58
1209 Geneva
Switzerland

TELEPHONE: + 41 22 733 43 30
FACSIMILE: + 41 22 734 55 62

UNITED KINGDOM

Nigel C. R. WILLIAMS, C.M.G.
Ambassador

Glyn WILLIAMS
First Secretary (WTO)

ADDRESS: Permanent mission of the United Kingdom
Rue de Vermont 37-39
1202 Geneva
Switzerland

TELEPHONE: + 41 22 918 23 00
FACSIMILE: + 41 22 918 23 33

UNITED STATES OF AMERICA

Booth GARDNER
Ambassador

ADDRESS: Permanent mission of United States of America

Avenue de la Paix 1-3
1202 Geneva
Switzerland

TELEPHONE: + 41 22 749 52 41
FACSIMILE: + 41 22 749 53 08

URUGUAY

Miguel BERTHET
Ambassador

ADDRESS: Permanent mission of Uruguay
Rue de Lausanne 65 (4th Floor)
1202 Geneva
Switzerland

TELEPHONE: + 41 22 732 83 66
FACSIMILE: + 41 22 731 56 50

UZBEKISTAN

Alisher SHAYKHOW
First Deputy Minister

ADDRESS: Ministry of Foreign Economic Relations of the
Republic of Uzbekistan
Buyuk Ipak Yuli St. 75
700 077 Tashkent
Uzbekistan

TELEPHONE: + 77 3712 39 41 71
FACSIMILE: + 77 3712 68 74 77 - + 77 3712 68 77 27

VANUATU

Roy M. JOY
Principal Trade Officer

ADDRESS: Department of Industry, Trade and Commerce

Government of Vanuatu
Private Mail Bag 030
Port Vila
Vanuatu

TELEPHONE: + 678 22 7770
TELEFAX: + 678 25 677

VENEZUELA

Alfredo TARRE MURZI
Ambassador
Juan Francisco MISLE GIRAND
Counsellor Minister (WTO)

ADDRESS: Permanent mission of Venezuela
               Chemin François-Lehmann 18a
               1218 Grand-Saconnex
               Switzerland

TELEPHONE: + 41 22 798 26 21 - + 41 22 798 26 23
FACSIMILE: + 41 22 798 58 77

VIETNAM

Le Luong Minh
Ambassador

ADDRESS: Permanent mission of Vietnam
               Chemin François-Lehmann 34
               1218 Grand-Saconnex
               Switzerland

TELEPHONE: + 41 22 798 24 85
FACSIMILE: + 41 22 798 07 24

YEMEN

Yahya H. GEGHMAN

Ambassador

ADDRESS: Permanent mission of Yemen
Chemin du Jonc 19
1216 Cointrin
Switzerland

TELEPHONE: + 41 22 798 53 33 - + 41 22 798 53 34
FACSIMILE: + 41 22 798 04 65

YUGOSLAVIA

Vladimir PAVICEVIC
Ambassador

ADDRESS: Permanent mission of Yugoslavia
Chemin Thury 5
1206 Geneva
Switzerland

TELEPHONE: + 41 22 839 33 44
FACSIMILE: + 41 22 839 33 59

ZAIRE

Marume MULEME
Ambassador

ADDRESS: Permanent mission of Zaire
Rue de Lausanne 45A-47A
Case Postale 2595
1211 Geneva 2
Switzerland

TELEPHONE: + 41 22 740 37 44
FACSIMILE: + 41 22 740 37 44

ZAMBIA

Patric N. SINYINZA

Ambassador

ADDRESS: Permanent mission of Zambia
Chemin du Champ-d'Anier 17-19
1209 Geneva
Switzerland

TELEPHONE: +41 22 788 53 30 - +41 22 788 53 31
FACSIMILE: +41 22 788 53 40

ZIMBABWE

JOKONYA Tichaona Joseph B.
Ambassador

ADDRESS: Permanent mission of Zimbabwe
Chemin William Barbey 27
1292 Chambésy
Switzerland

TELEPHONE: +41 22 758 30 11
FACSIMILE: +41 22 758 30 44